God Does Guide Us

God Does Guide Us

By

W. E. SANGSTER

HODDER & STOUGHTON
ST. PAUL'S HOUSE
LONDON, E.C.4

First printed . . . July *1934*

Reprinted . . November *1934*

Reprinted . . November *1936*

Reprinted . . February *1938*

PRINTED AND BOUND IN GREAT BRITAIN FOR HODDER AND STOUGHTON, LTD.,
BY RICHARD CLAY AND SONS, LTD., BUNGAY SUFFOLK.

TO

MY MOTHER

DEAR SOUL!

ὅσοι γὰρ πνεύματι θεοῦ ἄγονται,
οὗτοι υἱοὶ θεοῦ εἰσίν

Preface

THE GROUP MOVEMENT has put the word " guidance " on the lips of all reflective Christians and made it a topic of keen debate. No part of the technique which the Movement has developed has been more earnestly defended by its supporters or challenged by its critics.

The aim of this book is to explain and defend the " Group " view of guidance. In my opinion, one of the chief services which this new tide of spiritual life is rendering to Christian people, is to make them explore again their resources in God and to see more clearly the implications of the faith they hold. Consequently, I have drawn my illustrations from beyond the borders of the Movement in an effort to show that a simple faith in particular guidance is as old and as wide as the Church itself and not just, as some have suggested, the invention of modern enthusiasts.

I hope also that the book will serve, in its modest way, to contradict the reiterated charge that the supporters of the Group Movement have done no thinking.

My warm thanks are due to five of my friends. Mr. W. E. Smith, who, together with other constant help, has typed the MS. The Revs. Leslie D. Weatherhead, M.A., F. B. Roberts, and J. E. Mattinson, B.D., who have made useful suggestions. And to Mr. T. Cyril Ellams, who has read the proofs.

Several of the chapters have appeared as articles in the " Group's " magazine.

W. E. SANGSTER.

Scarborough, July 1934.

Contents

GOD IS NOT DUMB, THAT HE SHOULD SPEAK NO MORE

IN DIVERS MANNERS

PERPLEXED, BUT NOT IN DESPAIR

TEACH ME THY WAY, O LORD, AND LEAD ME IN A PLAIN PATH

GOD IS NOT DUMB, THAT HE
SHOULD SPEAK NO MORE

CHAPTER I

THE FACT

Thou shalt guide me with Thy counsel, and afterward
receive me to glory.—DAVID.

There are two great classes of people in the world of Christians to-day: (1) Those who have God's will in their
character; (2) Those who have God's will likewise in their
career.

Those who belong to the first class are really outside a
great part of God's will altogether. They understand the
universal part, they are moulded by it, and their lives as lives
are in some sense noble and true. But they miss the private
part, the secret whispering of God in the ear, the constant
message from heaven to earth.—HENRY DRUMMOND.

MANY things make it hard
to believe in the guidance of God. The study of the
stars makes it hard. The study of the rocks makes it
hard. And the grace of humility seems to make it harder
still.

When the astronomer turns away from his telescope
to tell us that the nearest star to the earth is probably
twenty-five billions of miles away, and that the total
number of stars in the universe is something like the
total number of grains of sand on all the sea-shores of the
world, our minds are terrified by such inconceivable
figures and prayer seems frozen.

When the geologist, reading the history of the rocks,
estimates the age of our world at some two thousand
millions of years, the threescore years and ten of our
human lives are less than the twinkling of an eye, and it
seems impossible to assert that such short-lived creatures
can hold fellowship with the vast mathematical mind

which lies behind the universe. Even to suppose it, appears absurd. In the bewildering vastness of space and peering down the long vistas of time, it seems so pitifully naïve to ask, " Does God care for *me* ? " " Is He interested in *my* doings ? " " Will He direct me in all the details of my little life ? " " Does He long for my poor heart ? " To many people such questions give their own answer, and it is (according to their temperament) a stoical, or despairing " No ! " The very questions themselves, they say, are a queer compound of fear and conceit, and the hope that lies in them is only fostered by the childish habit of building our thought of God around our thought of man. They concede that it may be both natural and forgivable to ask such questions, but the mature and masculine mind will not hesitate at a bleak answer, nor flatter itself with a false hope.

And yet we cannot leave the question there. It is not fear of truth but love of truth that will not call the matter closed. There is weighty evidence on the other side. Rich experience has made us witnesses to God's guidance. Neither the vastness of space, nor the everness of time, forecloses the discussion. Who made vastness a standard of value ? A baby is more than a mountain; a baby can *love*. A man is more than a star; a man can *think*. Nor is longevity the last word. A man is more than a tortoise even though it be true that the tortoise is the Methuselah of the animal kingdom. Astronomy and geology may conspire to prove the utter insignificance of man, but man is still the astronomer and the geologist. . . . He is something more. He is a child of God.

But let us look, for a moment, at the reasoning of those who feel that the affairs of the individual life are too trivial for God's notice, and who accuse those who believe in detailed guidance of thinking of God too humanly. We know how their objections run. " Can the great cosmic mind concern itself with trifles ? "

" Does God, ' who alone workest great marvels,' interest
Himself in the unimportant details of our insignificant
lives ? "   " Is it possible to believe that the Creator and
Sustainer of the Universe notices the need of separate
persons on this microscopic earth ? "   Modesty reproves
our faith and philosophers smile.   Santayana discovers
in Spinoza's message a reproof to all who claim this
guidance from God.   " It counsels us to say to those
little gnostics, to those circumnavigators of being : I
do not believe you ; God is great." [1]

But are we in need of such reproof ?   Is our thought
too human after all ?   Is it not nearer the truth to lay the
same charge against our critics ?   Surely it is because *they*
have built up *their* idea of God too closely on a human
model that they find it hard to believe that He can both
sustain the world and take a Father's care of His children.
Obsessed with the conviction that managing directors
leave details to subordinates, they are quietly scornful of
the idea that God's care runs down to trivialities.   But is
there ground for scorn, or even (at this point) for the
strain of faith ?   We hold to God's personal care not
in spite of His greatness but *because* of it.   Our thought of
God here is not too human ; the reasoning of our critics
is that.   He is not a smaller God who astounds the
astronomer with His mathematical universe, and at the
same time answers the cry of the burdened heart and speaks
peace to the penitent soul.   He is a greater God, such a
God as Jesus revealed and before whom the angels veil
their faces.   Though He is far, far above our thought,
we dare believe that He stoops to ask the love of our poor
hearts : though whirling worlds move at His word, we
dare believe that He said, " I will guide thee."   " Be
still and *know* that I am God."

Nor is this belief as daring as some would think.
Many witnesses speak in its confirmation.   For centuries
men have ventured on this faith, sought the promised

---

[1] *The Ethics of Spinoza*, Everyman's Library, p. xxii.

guidance, and testified that God was as good as His word. The Bible is full of such stories. Peep into the Old Testament. Think of Abraham's slave seeking Rebekah, or the stories of Moses, Samuel and the Prophets; old, colourful stories, many of them, and not without the marks of spiritual immaturity or the reminder that God's revelation grows, but all witnessing to a profound faith that God's guidance is particular as well as general, and willingly given to the limit of a man's capacity to understand. Or peep into the New Testament. Think of Philip and the Ethiopian, or of Ananias and Saul, or of Peter and Cornelius; all these stories are substantially false if God's guidance does not run down to what appear to be trivialities, and if He does not direct His devoted and trustworthy servants in the details of His will.

Or consider the supreme example of Jesus. No one can study the Gospels with any seriousness without realising how large a part of His time was given to prayer, nor how confidently He spoke of the will of God. " My meat is to do the will of Him that sent me." " If any man willeth to do His will, he shall know of the teaching, whether it be of God." In Gethsemane, though He breaks into a bloody sweat, He can still say, " Nevertheless, not as I will, but as Thou wilt." And he pressed this life of obedience on His followers, for He taught His disciples to pray, " Thy will be done "—a prayer which presupposes the possibility of *knowing* that will, and knowing it (one must assume), not as a gelatinous mass of vague sentiment, but with some concreteness and precision.

And all through the ages, men and women have claimed that God has condescended to guide them. Sometimes the witness appears in unexpected places. Consider, for instance, the testimony of the much-tried Robinson Crusoe! All adults who read his adventures marvel at his theological preoccupations and his sage comments on life and religion. He believed in guidance. He says :

" How wonderfully we are delivered when we know nothing of it; how, when we are in a quandary, as we call it, a doubt or hesitation whether to go this way or that way, *a secret hint* shall direct us this way when we intended to go that way, nay, when sense, our own inclination, and perhaps business, has called us to go the other way, *yet a strange impression upon the mind* . . . shall overrule us to go this way, and it shall afterwards appear that had we gone that way which we should have gone, and to our imagination ought to have gone, we should have been ruined and lost."

But if we find these things in a novel, what shall we find in the writings of the saints ? In each generation, godly men and women have claimed that the discipline of prayer has had this blessed fruit. Augustine and Luther, St. Teresa and Wesley—these, and countless others, vouch for its truth. Nor does our own age lack its witnesses. Consider George Müller of Bristol. William James says that Müller's prayers were of the " crassest petitional order," but few people can read the record and remain unimpressed. Müller had a profound faith in guidance. He said, in March 1895 :

" I never remember in all my Christian course, a period now of sixty-nine years and four months, that I ever sincerely and patiently sought to know the will of God by the teaching of the Holy Ghost, through the instrumentality of the word of God, but I have always been directed rightly."

After a lifetime of prayer, Samuel Chadwick asserted :

" The humblest followers of Jesus may know the divine will at first hand. It is every man's privilege to be fully assured in the will of God. The Divine attention to detail is amazing. Nothing is too trivial for Omniscience. Come straight to God. . . . Lay all questions naked before Him and He will make it plain to you what is His will." [1]

We may leave it at that. Many things about guidance are not clear to us. Some of them will yield to prayer and hard thinking, and concerning the rest we can only say that several of the richest experiences of life elude explanation. But, if we can begin our study by accepting the fact, and then pursue it with humility and patience, correlating the undeniable experience of others, and persisting in the practice of its simple technique, we shall know it for ourselves. Unquestionably. Beyond every semblance of doubt. The simplest among us can know. The least gifted may say, " Even *me*."

> " It is a thing most wonderful . . .
> . . . And yet I *know* that it is true."

---

[1] *The Path of Prayer*, Chadwick, pp. 79 f. (Hodder and Stoughton.)

CHAPTER II

THE WAY

I will bring the blind by a way that they knew not; I will lead them in paths that they have not known.—ISAIAH.

> Not for one single day
> Can I discern my way,
>   But this I surely know,—
> Who gives the day,
> Will show the way,
>   So I securely go.
>
> JOHN OXENHAM.

CYRUS, King of the Persians, was a worshipper of idols, but the Old Testament asserts that he was a chosen intrument of the Living God. It was to this magnificent pagan that the words were addressed, " I girded thee, though thou hast not known me," and Isaiah declares that, behind all his conquest and Empire-building, the purposes of Jehovah could be found. Unaware of it himself, he was being girded and guided by the Divine hand.

All true Christian people accept the fact of divine guidance, though some believe that the guidance is unconscious. We scheme and plan but we never fathom the eternal thought. We make our decisions in such twilight as we have, though we are often harassed by a sense of uncertainty at the time. It is not possible, they feel, to know the will of God with definiteness, on the really perplexing issues of life, until *after* the event. One must have faith to believe that God gets His way somehow. Illumination often comes at the last, but

> " Not till the hours of light return
> All we have built do we discern."

Phillips Brooks began life as a schoolmaster. It was his own deliberately chosen career and one in which both he and his friends expected him to do well. But he was a failure. In the Boston Latin School they remembered him as a kindly soul but as one incapable of keeping discipline. He returned home mortified beyond words. And then it was that the call to the ministry came to his greatly wondering mind, and he was led on step by step to a career of amazing influence as a preacher, and to a position of the highest esteem on both sides of the Atlantic. Looking back, Phillips Brooks felt that his false start wasn't a false start at all. He saw the purpose of God in it. Even when he remembered the humiliation, he could have said :

> " I'll bless the hand that guided,
> I'll bless the heart that planned."

It was simply the path thither, the path of necessary discipline and wise chastening of the spirit, and it brought him to the beginning of his real task equipped with the weakness that God converts into strength. He knew it was guidance, *when he looked back*.

Even the apparent exceptions to the rule are not always real exceptions. A man is sometimes a poor judge of his own work, and an unreliable witness to the element of guidance in it. Think of F. W. Robertson, the prophetic preacher of Brighton. He wanted to be a soldier, as his father and grandfather had been, and as his three brothers were. He says :

> " I was rocked and cradled to the roar of artillery and the very name of such things sounds to me like home. . . . I cannot see a regiment manœuvre, nor artillery in motion, without a choking sensation." [1]

But the commission, for which he had applied, was long delayed, and finally, though with great reluctance, he

[1] *Life and Letters of Rev. F. W. Robertson*, Stopford A. Brooke, p. 8. (Kegan Paul, Trench & Co.)

took his father's advice, and the advice of a friend, and matriculated at Brazenose as a preparation for taking orders. Five days later the commission came. Robertson's feelings can be imagined, but he accepted his father's judgment that God had directed the circumstances, and the commission was declined. He was long perplexed by it, the part his friend had played and the trivialities on which the decision seemed to turn. Among his papers, this relic of his perplexity was found

> " If I had not met a certain person, I should not have changed my profession; if I had not known a certain lady, I should not probably have met this person; if that lady had not had a delicate daughter who was disturbed by the barking of my dog, if my dog had not barked that night, I should now have been in the dragoons or fertilising the soil of India. Who can say that these things were not ordered ? . . ." [1]

Something of gloom and depression hangs over the fine story of Robertson's life. He was lonely : he was misunderstood. All his life he was oppressed with the thought that his ministry was a failure. When he looked back, it took an energetic effort of faith to see the guidance in it.

But nobody now thinks of his ministry in terms of failure, nor finds it hard to believe that his work lay in the realm of thought rather than in the realm of action. Eighty years after he preached them, his sermons still keep their place and men recognise in him the pioneer of a new era of theological thought. The guidance that seemed so uncertain when he was twenty-one had justified itself when his life came to an end at thirty-seven. What other achievements a man might have made had his choice of a career been other than it was is a vain speculation. Christian men will continue to believe

[1] *Life and Letters of Rev. F. W. Robertson*, Stopford A. Brooke, p. 13. (Kegan Paul, Trench & Co.)

that a life was guided which displays the spirit of Jesus, and finds scope for its abilities in the service of man. Phillips Brooks and F. W. Robertson found such scope in the Christian ministry. Other men have found it in other spheres of life. Deeply the Christian believes that beneath all the flux and change of this mortal life, God is seeking to work out a profound purpose. Many assert that He has a plan for every life, but still hesitate to believe that the guidance is ever communicated in a special way. God's path, they feel, can only be seen when you look *back*. Like a faint mountain track it often twists and turns and is hardly discernible when you are on it, but looking back from the valley it is a definite stripe on the hillside. In such a way, and only in such a way, many believe that the guiding hand of God can be seen. We are guided, but, hardly better than Cyrus, we have little or no awareness of it at the time.

But does this really exhaust all the aspects of divine guidance? Allowing that this is true in its degree, is it the *whole* truth? It does not cover all the instances of guidance given in the Bible. It ignores a wide, and growing, area of Christian experience. Moreover, it does not deal with the reality of the situation. Guidance, to be guidance in any satisfying sense at all, is required *before* the event. It should come in the hour of perplexity and carry some sense of assurance with it. Perhaps that is asking too much and denying one of the conditions of life as we have it here, namely, that faith and trust are at the heart of our existence and not sight and certitude.

But it cannot be denied that just such guidance is what our hearts cry out for. If " our wills are ours to make them Thine," we need to know what the will of God is. The people who say that we can see the hand of God when we look back, must not forget the many people who look back and cannot see any order or purpose in their life at all. Sir William Robertson Nicoll once remarked that he had been much impressed by the com-

mon conviction of his friends that they had been guided
in the big decisions of life, and that if they had to make the
decisions over again, would not have acted differently.
One cannot help remembering that Sir William always
chose his friends among successful men and, on the
witness of his daughter and nephew, seemed incapable
of recognising that some high quality in a man might
have been the hindrance to what the world calls success.[1]
A man who has done well for himself can look back on
his life with some content and talk about the hand of
the Divine Guide as seen in retrospect, but it would be a
strange mixing of the value of earth and heaven to assume
that a plenitude of this world's goods was a proof of God's
direction. Many look back and see no clear purpose
threading the years of their life, and sometimes they
wonder if they have missed the way. If prayer had had a
larger place in their life, would it have become two-way
prayer, and would God have been real? If God was
more real, would His way have been clearer in times of
perplexity? would the very circumstances of life have
revealed a hidden significance? would one's powers of
reason have been clarified? would the Bible have been a
more attractive and helpful volume? would the voice of
God through the Christian Fellowship have sounded
louder and more distinct?

The answer of this book is an emphatic " Yes " to all
those questions. God is able and willing to guide us far
more than the hesitant faith of many of His children has
yet made possible. The poverty of our spiritual lives;
our unwillingness to put a fence round some definite
portion of our day and keep it for Him; our unbelief
concerning His voice in the soul—all these have hampered
Him. It is not denied that with all our blindness He has
been able to guide us in some degree. But how much
more effectively could He counsel and direct us if faith
was really *expectant* and we listened as well as prayed.

[1] *William Robertson Nicoll*, Darlow, p. 420. (Hodder
and Stoughton.)

It is no part of the argument to imply that here is some infallible rule and that, within the compass of one small life, an unerring judgment can be reached on every problem as it arises. But it is argued that by consecration to God, faith in His willingness to direct us and devotion to His way of life, our spirits are sensitised in a marvellous way to His will and we are guided as never before. Everything may not be clear, but much more is clear now than was clear then. Trust is still at the heart of our religion, and reason is not atrophied. Nor can it be denied that perplexities still come. But the contrast between the darkened streets of London in war-time and the blaze of light which is now flung on every important thoroughfare is not sharper than the contrast between the path of life before one came to faith in real guidance, and now. One cannot study the lives of the saints without being impressed by their poise, the impression they give of power in reserve, and their ability to make great decisions without strain. They were sensitive to the guidance of God. When others were in a maze of conflicting policies, they seemed to *know* what to do.

To those who have no experience of this guidance, denial will seem easy. But it is perilous to deny anything on that ground alone. One is reminded of the little girl who thought that she had exhausted mathematics when she had learned the twelve-times table, and when her grandfather said, with a twinkle in his eye, " What's thirteen times thirteen ? " she turned on him with undisguised scorn and said, " Don't be silly, Grandpa : there's no such thing."

Some people deny the reality of guidance simply because they've never experienced it, never ventured on the faith, never submitted to the discipline of it, never listened in. But it is real. As real as God, and as free as His love.

Paul said, " We are ambassadors for Christ." No ambassador would accept office if his privileges were curtailed, and one of the most jealously guarded of all ambassadorial privileges is the right to one's own mail-bag. The mail-bag of the British Ambassador to America is sealed in London, and delivered at the Embassy in Washington without examination either by the Customs or postal authorities. The Ambassador cannot possibly represent the King unless he is guaranteed uninterrupted communication with him. He stands in the King's place : it is imperative that he know the King's mind.

It was a daring metaphor that Paul used when he said, " We are ambassadors for Christ," and if we may extend it to ourselves we can say that it carries this as a consequence. We must know the King's mind. We must be in uninterrupted communication with our Sovereign. We hold office in order to do His bidding and we cannot do it unless we know what it is.

Yet still the promise runs, " I am the Lord thy God which teacheth thee to profit, which leadeth thee by the way thou shouldest go." [1]

[1] Isaiah xlviii. 17.

CHAPTER III

THE TERMS

And ye shall seek Me, and find Me, when ye shall search for Me with all your heart.—JEREMIAH.

LADY TROUBRIDGE in *The Book of Etiquette* informs her readers what rules it is necessary to observe on presentation at Court. Not everybody, it seems, is entitled to the honour. But the wives and daughters of the following classes may aspire. The aristocracy; government officials; Members of Parliament; the county gentry; the town gentry; the professions; merchants, bankers and members of the Stock Exchange, and men engaged in commerce " on a large scale." Necessarily, a large section of the community must be left out.

Leave to attend is granted by the Lord Chamberlain, and the presentation is usually made by a near relation or a close friend. Such a service is regarded as a very great favour and one which many ladies do not hesitate to refuse. Anything in a person's past which might come to light afterwards and which the Lord Chamberlain might disapprove would have serious consequences for the lady making the presentation. So the risk is not willingly taken.

Dress, too, is very important—and very costly. Lessons in deportment are strongly advised for some. One's motor or carriage must have a footman on the box. At the Palace itself there is a Great Hall to cross and a Grand Staircase to climb; the period of waiting is spent in one of the saloons which a Gentleman-at-Arms closes with a gilt barrier as soon as it is full. Finally, the long-expected moment comes. It is soon over. With her train down, the lady crosses the Picture Gallery to the Presence Chamber. When in front of the King, an official calls her name. Two curtsies and two steps, and she passes to the other side of the Chamber. She has been presented at Court.

And now let us contrast that with attendance at the Court of Heaven and an audience with the King of Kings. All may come : no questions now of social standing or of commerce " on a large scale." No introductions are necessary : no seeker is hindered by lack of a friend willing to grant the favour and take the risk. The past need not prevent us though it be as murky as midnight, nor need one delay for deportment or dress. Now, as ever, the sacrifices of God are a broken spirit; a broken and a contrite heart He will not despise.

But the contrast does not end there. By that strange perversity of human nature, which values things not at their real worth but by their rarity, and thinks lightly of the most precious gifts because they are given to all, people will covet, and scheme for, an invitation from the Lord Chamberlain's office and take only a tepid interest in their open access to the Lord of Lords, the only Ruler of Princes. They need not study times : they can come when they will. It is not a contact of moments : they can linger as long as they like. It is more than a glance of recognition : it can be a fellowship rich with the intimacies of home. Yet, they neglect the privilege, and act as though the door was barred against them. Many make no use of prayer at all and others employ it only in the most casual and perfunctory way. Nothing about them suggests the audience chamber of a King. A few scamped sentences hastily gabbled through in the morning : a few more drowsily murmured (perhaps in bed !) at night. We are a long way from the details of dress and deportment now. A little courtesy would be welcome. " Irreverent and ineffective " sums most of it up. In no serious sense of the word is it prayer at all. "You might as well stand on a hill and talk to the moon," said Spurgeon, "as kneel down and hurry through the Lord's Prayer, and then think that you have prayed."

Let us inquire on what terms God condescends to speak to us and what common principles belong to the prayer life of all the saints. Some technique we will naturally expect. Many acute thinkers look upon the absence of a technique of the prayer life as being one of the chief weaknesses of modern Protestantism. The little that is said about the culture of the soul is so pitifully vague. Indeed, some are still so raw as to pour scorn on the need for discipline at all, and cling to the stupid illusion that one can grow a soul by just praying when one "feels like it." One can master nothing if one is the creature of whims. Discipline is essential. The saints of all communions, being also the saints of one Communion, have worked by a rule. The serious effort after holiness demands it—in Catherine Booth as well as in Thomas à Kempis. It could turn one alternately to laughter and tears, to find people fully admitting the need to set several hours aside daily to master shorthand or a foreign language, and blandly supposing that they can conquer sin and know God by a few sleepy moments at the end of the day.

Aim for a quiet time in the early morning. *Why the morning?* Well, the mind is rested and fresh, and the day is still before you. If it is *early* you will be free from interruption. Some people hate getting up early in the morning. Good. It is all the better discipline for that very reason: one need not defend all the rigours of asceticism and yet feel with Paul that there is need to buffet the body. Some people complain that they are not really *awake* in the early morning, even if they get up. A sponge under the cold tap will help. Get up! No charge of vagueness can be brought against this advice. Get up! "Make conscience of *beginning* the day with God," said Bunyan. And one of the best ways of beginning the day well is to begin it the night before. Earlier rising may require earlier retiring. Wesley is said to have left the company of Dr. Johnson because it was near his bed-time. He had an appointment with God at 4 a.m. and he would not risk the perils of over-sleeping for the greatest litterateur of the age.

A brief time of prayer at night can round the day off and help one to check the guidance with which the day began. It is of special value that our last thoughts be thoughts of trust and peace, that while we sleep the strange thought-processes of our unresting minds should all be occupied with higher things. But this must not be a substitute for the morning watch. Theory and experience combine to stress the importance of the morning hour.

How long shall one spend in devotions in the morning ? Some people find an hour all too short, but our temperaments cannot be entirely ignored in this matter, and experience shows that different circumstances and different dispositions have their effect even here. Fifteen minutes, in the early morning, seems to fit some people to start the day, but if one begins with so brief a period of unhurried quiet, one should aim to make up an hour before the day is sped. Francis Asbury rose at five o'clock and spent his first hour in prayer. Newman was astir at the same time and was occupied with his devotions till he went to breakfast at eight. Andrew Bonar said, " Unless I get up to the measure of at least two hours in *pure prayer* every day I shall not be satisfied." In the light of all this, is it too much to ask for *one* hour a day for our devotions ? When one remembers how much time is spent in the average life on trifles, the request will not seem unreasonable. It may be taken as a minimum for any serious endeavour. If, on reflection, it still seems too much, it would be well to go back to the Valley of Decision and question the quality and completeness of your consecration. To make free use of the word " guidance," with no such background of daily devotion, is to misapply a precious and awesome term, and to bring it into disrepute. God does not treat us as dictaphones. His guidance is given on conditions. He has guided seekers and saints in every age, but, with all the variations of circumstances, their quest and conquest had this in common—they gave God time, and it becomes ever clearer that if we give God time, He will give us eternity.

How shall the time be spent? Almost certainly, with the Bible first. George Müller regarded that simple piece of method as one of the most useful discoveries he had made in fifty years. For the first ten years of his discipleship it was his custom, after having dressed in the morning, to go straight to prayer. But the results were somewhat disappointing and he came to abandon this direct stride to intercession. He says:

" I often spent a quarter of an hour, or half an hour, or even an hour on my knees before being conscious to myself of having derived comfort, encouragement or humbling of soul; and often, after having suffered much from wandering of mind for the first ten minutes, or a quarter of an hour, or even half an hour, I only then began *really to pray*. I scarcely ever suffer now in that way."

What made the difference? Simply this. He began with the New Testament.

" The first thing I did, after having asked in a few words the Lord's blessing upon His precious Word, was to begin to meditate on the Word of God, searching, as it were, into every verse. . . . The result I have found to be almost invariably this, that after a very few minutes my soul has been led to confession, or to thanksgiving, or to intercession, or to supplication; so that though I did not, as it were, give myself to *prayer*, but to *meditation*, yet it turned almost immediately more or less into prayer." [1]

[1] *The Autobiography of George Müller*, p. 153. (Nisbet.)

It does! Beginning our quiet time with the Book brings us swiftly into the conscious presence of God. Mind wandering is largely prevented and prayer is made easy. The Book first, then—with all its astonishing illumination. Prayer next—in all its manifold aspects : confession, adoration, intercession, petition. And then —the listening side of prayer : the quiet waiting upon God for the impression of His Will on our minds : this is the most discussed part of all the simple technique that the Goup Movement has developed, and the part with which we are most concerned here.

Of its importance there can be no doubt. If God condescends to speak to us by direct impressions upon the mind—as well as through the Bible, the Fellowship, and by other means more freely acknowledged—it is of the utmost consequence that we learn how best to receive His messages and how to be sure that they are His. But it will suffice, for the moment, if we are clear as to what form the method takes. It is easily caricatured. Even those who claim to practise it sometimes set it in a strange light, and speak of their " guidance " with distressing glibness. But the honest seeker for truth will have only one question in his mind, " What is the method at its best ? " " Can it really be called the guidance of God ? "

Still in the spirit of prayer, and with his mind open towards God, the disciple takes his notebook and pencil, and writes down certain thoughts that come to him. States of mind are not easily analysed or described, but it will serve at this point to say that it is not a definite meditation—*most* valuable though meditation is—nor yet is it an effort to " keep the mind blank." In the awesome and humbling sense of God's nearness and with a mind all compacted of prayer to know His Will, the surrendered and disciplined servant makes a record of the thoughts that come.

Completely passive he does claim to be, but consciously gives a certain direction to his thought. He goes over the previous day, in the white light of God, and tests himself by Christ's ethical standards. He does not think it ludicrous to make a note of the disapprovals of conscience, or the swift counsel of God when it speaks of restitution. He remembers the words of Christ : " If thou bring thy gift to the altar, and there rememberest that thy brother hath aught against thee; leave there thy gift before the altar, and go thy way; first be reconciled to thy brother, and then come and offer thy gift." [1] Remembering at the altar ! ! Isn't that just where one does remember ? One can forget in the busy world, and find it easy to be unmindful of the hasty words and hasty judgments one has used—but by the private altar, where one kneels in quiet with God, one *remembers*. The disciple makes a note of any guided restitution, a word of apology here and a letter of explanation there, and tries to heal immediately a wound he may have made.

Any particular problem which is on his heart he spreads out before God, and seeks to see it as God does, and to know the Divine mind about it. People for whom he has a particular concern he holds up before the loving Father, and listens lest, by some service or witness, he must be the means of answering his own prayers. Occasionally he reviews his personal weaknesses, and measures the progress he is making against them.

When the quiet time is over, he has notes of certain things to be done during the day, appointments to fix and letters to write. Not all of them have arisen out of his directed thought. Sometimes the inner voice has not merely responded to the questions reverently put, but has spoken a special word in the soul, and the disciple feels that he has a particular commission.

How can he tell if any of this is God's guidance ? Is he not exposing himself to the possibility of evil sug gestion or to the vagaries of his own imagination ?

To that question we must turn next.

[1] Matt. v. 23 f.

CHAPTER IV

THE VOICE

And the sheep hear His voice: and He calleth His own sheep by name, and leadeth them out. . . . And the sheep follow Him: for they know His voice.—St. John.

Blessed is the soul which heareth the Lord speaking within her, and receiveth from His mouth the word of consolation. Blessed indeed are those ears which listen not after the voice which is sounding without, but for the truth and teaching within.—Thomas à Kempis.

In the first scene of Bernard Shaw's *Saint Joan*, Captain Robert de Baudricourt argues with Joan about her mission and pours scorn on her claims to hear the heavenly voices.

Robert. How do you mean? voices?

Joan. I hear voices telling me what to do. They come from God.

Robert. They come from your imagination.

Joan. Of course. That is how the messages of God come to us.

Is that the answer to the question which puzzles us? Is the secret hint, that has so strangely and wonderfully led us, simply the fruit of our imagination? We cannot believe it. For a dozen different reasons, the answer fails of adequacy. Let us look for a moment at one of those reasons.

Men and women who have long made a practice of listening to God claim that they can distinguish between their own imagination and the impress of God's will. This claim is made quite deliberately, by servants of

B   33

God in all branches of the Universal Church, and in all centuries. They do not claim that this gift fell upon them suddenly. It is the product of long practice in the art of listening and they commend such constant practice to all who would qualify for the gift. The Quakers (who greatly stress this inner light) stress also the development in our power to perceive it. In the first part of the *Friends' Book of Discipline* we read :

" Our power to perceive the light of God is, of all our powers, the one which we need most to cultivate and develop. As exercise strengthens the body and education enlarges the mind, so the spiritual faculty within us grows as we use it in seeing and doing God's Will." [1]

God has sometimes spoken clearly to men who had no rich background of devotional life, but the rule still holds that those who would cultivate the power to know His voice must set time aside specifically for it, and set it aside every day.

Nor do those who claim this power deny that they are sometimes mistaken. Francis Herbert Stead, whose impressive witness to this gift we shall need to quote in a moment, admits the possibility of error. He says :

" I frankly confess that there was one impression, which I took to be an Assurance, which brought with it the sense of certainty and an infinite tenderness in its source and which had the other marks of a sure Word from Above. I rested my whole weight on it for some ten months. And then it was finally, irre-trievably falsified by the event. My faith was terribly shaken by the result. But it was not shattered. I recognised that this mistaken Assurance was not the basis of any practical mandate; it influenced action only negatively and even that scarcely at all. Very strong feeling was linked with it, and perhaps uncon-

[1] *Christian Life, Faith and Thought*, pp. 83 f. (Friends' Bookshop.)

sciously distorted my mental apparatus. And, after all, out of all the many Assurances which I have received, this was the only failure of any importance. A single exception of this kind would not be taken to discredit physical wireless. It ought not to be allowed to discredit spiritual wireless." [1]

There is the possibility of error in all things human—or *partly* human—but the adventurous soul will not turn back because of that. One would need to abandon life if one wished to avoid the very chance of error.

And there is so much to encourage us in the pursuit of this prize : so many witnesses come forward in its confirmation and so much positive testimony accumulates even among those who were hesitant to believe. Listen to Augustine speaking of his saintly mother Monica. Monica had been praying about a certain matter and seemed not to get the answer, and Augustine says :

" She saw, indeed, certain vain and imaginary things, such as the vehement desire of the human heart might conjure up; and these she told me about, not with her usual confidence when Thou hadst shown her anything, but slighting them. *For she could, she declared, through some feeling which she could not express in words, discern the difference between Thy revelations and the dreams of her own spirit.*" [2]

And now let us leap across the centuries and hear the same confident note in a modern writer, Mrs. Herman, whose little book, *Creative Prayer*, so richly deserves its increasing influence. I quote the passage in full, both for its vivid beauty and for its clear expression of the certainty and discipline of guidance :

" The alert and courageous soul making its first venture upon the spiritual life is like a wireless operator

[1] *The Unseen Leadership*, F. Herbert Stead, p. xi. (The Book Institute, Inverness.)

[2] *Confessions of St. Augustine*, Book VI, chap. xiii.

on his trial trip in the Pacific. At the mercy of a myriad electrical whispers, the novice at the receiver does not know what to think. How fascinating they are, these ghostly pipings and mutterings, delicate scratchings and thin murmurs—and how confusing! Now he catches the plaintive mutterings of a P. & O. liner trying to reach a French steamer, now the silvery tinkle from a Japanese gunboat seeking its shore station. There are aimless but curiously insistent noises, like grains of sand tumbling across tar paper : these are the so-called ' static ' noises of the atmosphere adjusting itself to a state of electrical balance. Again, there come series of tuneless splashings—that is heat-lightning miles away—followed by the rumour of a thunderstorm in the opposite direction. Now he thinks he has got his message, but it is only the murmured greetings of ships that pass in the night. And then, just as his ear has begun to get adjusted to the weird babel of crossing sounds, there comes a remote and thrilling whisper that plucks at his taut nerves and makes him forget all his newly-acquired knowledge. It is the singing of the spheres, the electrical turmoil of stars beyond the reach of the telescope, the birth-cry and death-wail of worlds. And when he is steeped soul-deep in the spell of this song of songs, there comes a squeaking, nervous spark, sharp as the squeal of a frightened rat. He decides to ignore it, and then suddenly realises that it is calling the name of his own boat. It is the expected message, and he nearly missed it !

" So the soul that waits in silence must learn to disentangle the voice of God from the net of other voices—the ghostly whisperings of the subconscious self, the luring voices of the world, the hindering voices of misguided friendship, the clamour of personal ambition and vanity, the murmur of self-will, the song of unbridled imagination, the thrilling note of religious romance. To learn to keep one's ear true in so subtle a labyrinth of spiritual sound is indeed at once a great adventure and a liberal education. *One hour of such listening may give us a deeper insight into the mysteries of human nature, and a surer instinct for Divine values, than a year's hard study or external intercourse with men."* [1]

And let us consider, finally, the testimony of Francis Herbert Stead. Those who are disposed to wave guidance aside as mystical and impractical would do well to notice to what fine social service his guidance led him. He tells the story in *The Unseen Leadership*, and it concerns (among other things) the initiation of the Hague Peace Conferences, Old Age Pensions, Slum Clearance, and the service of the Unemployed. Mr. Stead makes the same definite claim to distinguish between the vagaries of his own imagination and the impressions of God's Will. He says :

" Ever and again we found ourselves most thoughtfully directed from the Unseen : and when we were at our wits' end, the Gracious Bidding came. I venture to claim, after thirty years' experience, that I know the difference between a course that merely commends itself to my ordinary judgment or desire and is attended with no higher certainty, and a course which I am commanded to take. Everyone knows the difference between the conclusions of prudence or of rational deliberation, and the short, swift imperatives of conscience. A similar but greater difference divides one's own decisions from the peremptory commands of the Higher Will. And the decisive impact is further confirmed by the convergence of unforeseen circumstances." [2]

[1] *Creative Prayer*, E. Herman, pp. 70 ff. (James Clarke & Co., Ltd.)
[2] *The Unseen Leadership*, F. Herbert Stead, p. 43.

All this is weighty testimony. It spans the centuries and is born out of circumstances infinitely varied and comes from people of widely different ecclesiastical views. These witnesses are, moreover, simply typical of many others who claim humbly but quite definitely that they *can* distinguish between the flight of their imagination and the impress of God's Will. All confess the difficulty of expressing the difference, but affirm it just the same. It is like the voice of conscience and yet richer in positive content. It does not merely approve and disapprove : it informs and instructs. It cuts through a maze of jumbled ideas, gives insight into the needs of others, strips the cloak from crude ambition, pierces like a searchlight to the very heart of motives, exposes in a flash all the specious rationalisation of desire, and sweeps away, in a moment, the dozen different arguments with which we have sought to buttress the object of self-will. And the word it speaks is often peremptory and always authoritative. Like conscience, it carries its own sense of authority with it. The trained ear recognises the Divine Word and says with the Prophet, " Thus saith the Lord."

Not every day is the voice equally clear. The closeness of our walk with God determines that—and the Divine awareness of our need. Encouragement in the plain path of normal duty is our daily fare. Yet, again and again, the special word speaks clearly in the soul and the adoring disciple is reassured that all his way is overshadowed of the Lord. Jesus said that His sheep *know* His Voice. They do. Thousands more are learning to know it at this very time. The art of listening is being rediscovered in our own generation.

" I have never heard that Voice," says a disciple, " and I have prayed." But have you persisted in prayer and have you prayed *believing* that God will speak to you ? It is possible to pray, and pray often, with no such sense of expectation. The listening side of prayer has been strangely neglected. Many people fill every moment of their devotions by talking themselves. No real fellowship is possible under such circumstances. It is so pitifully one-sided. Common courtesy requires, at any time, that we listen as well as speak, and a sense of need and reverence ought to keep us silent and attentive in the presence of God. Only those who have practised this quiet waiting upon Him are qualified to speak of its truth.

But isn't it a rather dangerous doctrine to preach? Well, yes, it is. Yet it is not half so dangerous as living an unguided life. And, after all, knives are dangerous. People misuse them. Sometimes, in anger, they wound others with them and sometimes, by accident, they cut themselves. Yet, nobody advocates the prohibition of knives. Their wise use has made them an indispensable tool of man.

People have sometimes claimed that the Voice of God had urged them to an action that we positively know He would not commend, and even those who listen most intently for Him admit their liability to error. But we cannot abandon so precious a privilege because some have sophistically used it as a plea for their own will, or because others, with the best intentions, have made occasional mistakes.

We would warn the immature disciple against too positive an assertion that he knows the voice of God. We would remind him that God's will is not in dispute in certain broad areas of basic morality and we would encourage him to apply the other tests of guidance as well. But we do hold up before him the plain possibility and the dear hope of disentangling the Voice of God from all the other clamorous voices that speak within the soul of man, and of knowing that the Blessed Lord is directing his path. It is one of the most glorious things about our human nature. Only to *imagine* it true is wonderful, but to be *sure* is very heaven.

To return, for a moment. Mr. Stead stated that his certitude concerning the Voice of God was confirmed

by " the convergence of unforeseen circumstances."
All who listen to God know what he means. Strange
coincidences attend one's path. Unexpected doors
open. One constantly feels that one is working with
Another. What should our attitude to these coincidences be ? Are they true confirmations ? Should we
look for them and treasure them up ? That question
must claim our consideration next.

IN DIVERS MANNERS

CHAPTER V

THROUGH CIRCUMSTANCES

I belong to a race and nature comprehending all human beings, yet I feel myself to be different from them all, and to require a treatment and guidance special to myself. God sees and knows me as a work of His own hands, altogether distinct from all His other works. He intends me to fill a place which no other creature can fill, and is dealing with me in accordance with this special individuality. Thus I feel myself, as it were, alone with God. He only fully understands me, and He meets my need, according to His full understanding of me, by a course of circumstances chosen for my own personal education by His fatherly love and wisdom. It seems to me that He meets my actual condition at each successive moment, so that I do not feel as though I were put under a law in order to undergo a certain process, but as face to face continually with One who is watching every change that comes over my spirit as much as if He had nothing else to care for in the universe, and who varies His dealings with me in accordance with those changes. He is thus *my* God and Father as well as *our* God and Father.—THOMAS ERSKINE OF LINLATHEN.

HERE are three stories, taken almost at random from a host of similar stories and quoted simply to bring us quickly to the question, Is Guidance confirmed by the convergence of unforeseen circumstances?

The first is told by Dr. Alfred T. Schofield, the well-known Harley Street specialist. Some years ago, Dr. Schofield persuaded a friend of his, a lady holding an important position on the staff of a leading evening newspaper, to attend a meeting at Torrey's Gospel Tent in the Strand. The lady, who was a convinced Christian, though a rather ineffective one, kept the appointment and was given a seat on the platform next to the Japanese Ambassador. The address that evening was particularly dull, and in her report to the newspaper the lady said that she had not had a single thrill. And yet the meeting haunted her. She had felt a strange power in it that followed her home and made her miserable at the thought of her powerless life. Finally, she picked up the Bible and read a book right through and then knelt down to pray, and as she prayed the word " Horn " came to her. " Horn, Horn, Horn." Nothing but "Horn." She went to sleep at last with the same word sounding in her ears.

Next morning, at the office, she asked a clerk if he knew anybody of the name of " Horn," and the clerk came back later to say that the only " Horn " he could find was spelt with an " e " and was Sylvester Horne, the pastor of Whitefield's Mission in Tottenham Court Road. So the lady wrote to Sylvester Horne and asked him if there was any Christian work that she could do at the Mission, and he wrote back describing her offer as " most remarkable." He and his deacons had been in earnest prayer for weeks for someone to teach a large class of young ladies from the big stores of Maple's and Shoolbred's, and he could only regard her offer as an answer to their prayers. So the door of service opened and the lady stepped quickly through.

The next story carries us to America and to the office of Sam M'Clure, the editor and publisher. M'Clure was endeavouring to run a magazine on somewhat novel lines and finding the going hard. One day he was down to his last farthing and felt himself to be on the edge of bankruptcy. Only swift and generous help could save him. He dropped on his knees on the office floor and prayed for that help. Nor had the day ended before it came. An Englishman, who was only a mere acquaintance, walked into his office and said, " M'Clure, I believe in you and in the future of your magazine," and put

£1000 on the table. The Englishman was Arthur Conan
Doyle. The £1000 was the entire proceeds of his first
American tour and money that he could ill afford. But
he obeyed the strange impulse to carry the money to
M'Clure though he knew nothing of his urgent need.
Both M'Clure and Conan Doyle have told the story each
from his own angle and in complete confirmation of the
other's account, and both looked back on the incident
as an astonishing instance of the power of prayer.

The third story concerns the writer. I have made it
a practice of my quiet time to ask God's guidance in all
areas of my life and ministry, not to the atrophy of reason
but to the overruling of it in any way where it runs
counter to the Divine Will. Particularly do I seek
guidance in my pastoral work : where to call and how
to make best use of the personal contacts of the home.
One must work to a plan in this, as in other things,
and yet beware lest the plan become a prison and make
one deaf to a special word from God.

One morning as I waited quietly before God, it was
borne in upon me that I must call on a certain woman
that day. I resisted the thought. It did not fit in with
my plans. I knew no reason why I should go to her
home. To go in that direction would mean one call ;
to go the way I had planned would mean a dozen. Yet
her name dinned in my ears and I went. And the
memory of that visit will always be sweet to me. I
can see her wan face as I write. Bewilderment and
delight both had a place on it. "Do come in," she
said, and when I sat down she added, "Fancy you
remembering."

But I had remembered nothing and said so. And then
she reminded me. "It was a year ago to-day," she said,
"since you buried my husband. I have been dreading
this day and got up this morning fearfully overwrought
and feeling that I must run away from the house and
every stabbing memory. But, as I tried to pray, God
came very near and seemed to urge me to wait within

the home. Somehow I *knew* He would send me a word of comfort." So we talked together quietly and confidently of the Blessed Hope—the sure and *certain* hope (sublime paradox !)—and I reminded her again that *I* had not remembered but that God had sent me. And my forgetfulness seemed a little thing to her at the thought that He was mindful. "It is very wonderful," she said; "God must keep a calendar."

Well, there are the three stories. Let it be borne in mind that they are typical of hundreds of others and have not been selected because they have any specially striking features. Let it be remembered that most people who pray have had *some* experience of singular leading, and that those who deeply believe God guides His children in details and who seek His direction in the doings of every day can point to many strange happenings hardly a whit less remarkable than the three instances we are considering. What is our judgment on all these stories ? Are they true ? And, if they are true, are they just odd little occurrences, or do they tell us something profoundly important about the Will of God and the way He works ?

There are, I think, three possible answers open to us. We can doubt the evidence. We can say that the events did not occur just as their narrators say they did and that they are exaggerating to the glory of God (!). Or we can say that they are just coincidences. Coincidences are common enough in the world and come to people who have no interest in religion at all. Or we can accept their own explanation and say that a purposeful and loving mind lies behind the seeming chaos of circumstance, and that when God is operating through surrendered lives He can effect His great desire and work all things together for good. There is, perhaps, another possible explanation open to us. We can turn to telepathy for a solution and borrow psychic terms with which to hint at our meaning. But it will hardly be an *explanation*. We know too little of these subjects to explain our problems by their aid, and if further research on these lines does give us the clue that we seek, it will not exclude God from the process. After a period of doubt upon the point, our fathers came to see that if they accepted the evolutionary hypothesis they would not shut God out of creation but simply show the way by which He worked. We can profitably remember the same thing in all efforts to explain guidance on telepathic lines. If they succeed they will simply show the way by which God works. To some people psychology may seem to provide a satisfactory explanation, and the personal experience quoted above will seem to them to be a clear instance of " unconscious " memory, and a further proof of the astonishing power of the " unconscious " to register time. But, again, it will but show the way in which God works and come under the third possible answer that we have distinguished.

Let us look then at each of those answers in turn. Can we trust the evidence ? Are the stories substantially true ? In the great majority of cases there can be little doubt that they are. Even if we allow for the tendency of some minds to magnify the miraculous and recast all their experiences until they make them into marvels, we cannot dispose of any serious proportion of the instances in that way. Too many with a bias *against* belief in God's detailed guidance have been constrained by the evidence to accept it. Some have had the interesting and humiliating experience of arguing against the very *possibility* of it and then—in answer to the most tremulous essay in faith—proved it for themselves.

Are they just coincidences ? Coincidences are, of course, common enough. Things occur every week which no novelist, with a concern for his reputation, would put in a book. He would fear to be accused of stretching the long arm of coincidence too far. And yet they occur. Are all these stories of " guidance " nothing but coincidence ? The difficulty of that explanation is this. There are *so many* of these instances to explain and they have a definite *coherence*. Pure coincidences almost always have an " odd " character. They happen —but it would be difficult to discover even a freakish " purpose " in them, nor does one strange coincidence have any kind of relation to another. But in the company of those who wait on God for guidance one story finds many parallels and, when all the experience has been pooled, one cannot resist the conclusion that a purposeful mind is moving behind it to a definite end. Professor Bernard Bosanquet in *The Essentials of Logic* tells of the doubt he felt in the judgment of his antiquarian friends when they showed him a few misshapen pieces of flint and declared that they were primitive tools.[1] A casual glance at two or three examples gave no justification for the theory. The suggestion seemed fantastic. But when Bosanquet saw the fine collection of flints in the Blackmore Museum—the same features repeated again and again in a hundred different specimens—his doubts disappeared. Clearly they were man-made with a purposeful mind behind them.

It is not dissimilar with these stories of guidance. Glance at one or two of them and you may not feel constrained to accept the suggestion that God is behind them. Imagination or coincidence will seem a much more natural explanation. But study a hundred instances, the experience of people who were neither expecting nor desiring the miraculous and on whose ability to give an exact account of what occurred it would be a vulgar offence to cast a doubt, and you will find it wellnigh impossible to resist the conclusion that these events give impressive evidence that we are working with Another. Clearly they are God-given with a purposeful mind behind them. God is at work in His world in things small and great. It pleases some people to say that His work can only be seen in its broad aspects : the slow unfolding of great purposes that

[1] *The Essentials of Logic*, Bosanquet, p. 143.

span the ages. But it isn't true. The microscope gives as emphatic witness to the wonder of creation as the telescope, and the details of God's dealing with individuals show His watchful care over His world as much as the mightiest purpose He entertains. God guides. Events prove it. What we have felt and seen with confidence we tell.

A dozen other questions leap to our lips. Why is the guidance not always clear? Why don't these secret hints come to everybody? If they occur sometimes, why not always? But we must leave these questions for the moment. The whole problem of unanswered prayer is involved in them; God's respect for our personality; His response to our need rather than our prayers; the difficulty of the third will; our incomplete surrender. But of this we can be sure : our lack of faith and our sloth in prayer will account for a great deal of our deafness. How often has He spoken and we have not heard! Preoccupied. Too busy for God. Hurrying here and there in our breathless way, supposing that we are only serving our cause when we are *doing* things.

It will be time enough to face the bigger problems of the subject when the curable ones have received attention and when, by full surrender, trustful listening and swift obedience, we have put it to the test ourselves.

CHAPTER VI

THROUGH REASON

Religious people seem to be losing some of their faith in prayer; they think it scientific not to pray in the sense of simple petition. They may be right; it may be the highest attitude never to seek for anything specific, only for acquiescence. If saints feel so, they are undoubtedly right, but so far as ordinary science has anything to say to the contrary, a more childlike attitude might turn out truer, more in accordance with the total scheme.—Sir Oliver Lodge.

> Lord, that I may learn of Thee,
> Give me true simplicity;
> Wean my soul and keep it low,
> Willing Thee alone to know.
>
> Let me cast my reeds aside,
> All that feeds my knowing pride,
> Not to man, but God submit,
> Lay my reasonings at Thy feet.
>
> Charles Wesley.

Most people who are interested in guidance are perplexed as to its relationship with reason, and many of the warnings given to believers are concerned with the need to respect thought.

Nor need we resent the warnings—even though some of them are very naïve and appear to be addressed to morons. Reason is one of the highest of the human endowments, and God cannot wish that His priceless gift become atrophied for want of use. More thought—and not less—is clearly the urgent need of the age. It is one of the cardinal misfortunes of the times that people seem content to catch the epidemic opinion, or buy it for a penny in a newspaper, rather than undertake the labour of thinking it out for themselves. Religion is not the handmaid of shoddy thinking. It has discovered no by-pass road to all knowledge that shall cut out the need for careful and laboured thought. Guidance is a glorious and precious privilege, which insulates one from worry; but does not deliver one from the moil of mental stress. Reason we must. Are we not called upon to love the Lord our God with all our *mind*? We cannot think that God can be fittingly served by people who have become intellectually effete.

And yet unaided reason is often a disappointing tool. The hymn-writer calls it a " glimmering ray." Burns reminds us that " the best laid schemes o' mice an' men gang aft a-gley." All of us have had the experience of putting our hardest and most patient thought into a thing, and then making a mistake in the end. It is unlikely that we shall ever win a full exemption from that peril while we live on this plane, but if, in the providence of God, our best thought can be helped by some special insight, or our reasoning lifted into a realm where the mystery of our motives is a mystery no more and where we can see with clearness what purposes are really influencing our conduct, then we are more likely to act with *true* reason and may find that there is no ultimate conflict between the reasonable and the right. But is there such a special insight? Is there any way in which we can reason *with* God, or so submit the fruit of our thought to His judgment that we can see where the Divine approval rests? The saints have always held that there is. They have not claimed for it an utter infalli-bility, but they are so sure of the difference it makes to the reasoning process that they describe the contrast as a stumbling in the twilight beside a striding forward in the sunshine. All sorts of metaphors are used in its descrip-tion. Charles Wesley puts it in his own way and prays for wisdom to " lay my reasonings at Thy feet."

Let us look at one or two instances in order to see how

this effort to lay our reasonings at God's feet might issue in a changed decision. A ministerial friend recently received a " call " to another church and he gave the invitation deep and prolonged thought. Reason opposed reason in his mind. Clearly he would have the opportunity of wide usefulness in his new sphere, hard as it would be to leave a people he had learned to love. His stipend would be appreciably more if he moved, and he remembered that this would mean that he would have more to give away. He had long held that the worst thing about being poor was that one had so little to share with other people. The new appointment would admit him also to a coveted academic circle and he was most anxious for any opportunity of enriching his mind. The preacher must be a scholar, he thought. His wife and children would benefit as well. They had missed a good many desirable things because, in obedience to an imperious call, he had chosen this impecunious life. Now those things might be made up a little. His wife would have wide scope for her social gifts, and the new circumstances would be ideal for the kiddies' education. It would hurt to leave, but still . . . the *reason* of the thing pointed to acceptance. He prepared to send an affirmative reply.

And then it was that the thought occurred to him that the decision had been too *personal*. He had worked it out almost alone. He had prayed about it in a rather perfunctory way and sought the Divine approval of a decision that he had already made. He would copy Wesley's example and lay his reasonings at God's feet. After some hours of meditation and prayer he spread it out before God, without prejudice or special pleading, and his mind was made up very soon. He decided to stay where he was. Speaking of the experience afterwards, he said, " Most of my ' reasons ' for going were simply burnt up. The question of stipend seemed despicable. God had provided hitherto. I would trust Him to provide for the future. The idea of getting more, to give more, was sheer sophistry in *me*. I have never had the grace of giving, and a wider margin would only make a larger problem. The academic ambitions fared no better. In the light of God, I could plainly see that intellectual pride fostered the thought. When I asked myself if such concentration on abstract study was the best use of *my* time, and most likely to serve me in the practical ministry, I couldn't feel that it was. Hour for hour, I felt that other reading and work would make more directly for the saving and serving of souls. As for the gains that would accrue to my wife and children, I saw in that hour that they were not only exaggerated but that it was simply my own selfishness, once removed. It was what *I* wanted, made to seem unselfish by being attached to my dependents. One question burned itself on my brain as I laid this problem out before God : ' Where can you do the most good ? ' and the answer to that question, taken by itself, did not seem so very hard and I decided to stay. My decision is neither quixotic nor eccentric. It is completely reasonable, as I see reason in the light of God."

That is one way in which we may pass from *our* reasons to *His* reasons, and change our mind.

But that instance will not answer all the problems, though the principle at the heart of it will answer a good many. Oftentimes the marrow of the matter is not a question of mixed motives at all : it is a question of fact. All human reasoning is honeycombed with uncertainty. We are seldom in possession of all the facts relating to the matter in the past and present, and, as to the future, the wisest among us can only guess. Hence, it should not surprise us if the constraint of guidance is sometimes towards a course for which it is impossible to give a completely valid reason. How can it be otherwise unless we assume that omniscience is a human attribute as well as a divine one ? Facts are known to God which are necessarily hidden from men. The disciple believes that God guides in the light of these facts, and it would surprise him if His guidance did not sometimes include the element of the unaccountable. But having learned, with some skill, to distinguish the constraint of the Spirit, he follows the leading, though the reason of it may not be obvious. Dr. J. Rendel Harris says that " the best proof we could have that the restraining or constraining power, that we find asserting itself in our lives, was *not* of God, would lie in the fact that its dictates always and at once secured our rational approbation." [1] So we believe. We freely admit that we follow a course, at times, for which we have no completely rational explanation, but we have high Apostolic authority for the practice, and we have many times enjoyed the complete confirmation of subsequent events.

But let us take an illustration from the Bible. In the sixteenth chapter of Acts we read of Paul journeying through the region of Phrygia and Galatia and being " *forbidden* of the Holy Ghost to speak the word in Asia." That, in itself, is astonishing. Paul *forbidden* to preach the Word. He would have been hard put to, to give a rational explanation of that.

So he planned to go into Bithynia, a rich and fertile province lying away to the north-east. One cannot imagine that the decision was lightly made. Paul would have given much thought to it. He had the mind of a missionary-statesman and judged this unevangelised area to be important. But when they turned their face in that direction " the Spirit of Jesus suffered them not." It is clear that the Apostle would not agree with those who say that no individual can be certain of the pressure of God's guiding hand. So they journeyed on to Troas, in ignorance of their real destination, and at no point of the journey, since leaving Iconium, could Paul have given a satisfactory reason for his course or his silence. But at Troas a vision came to him (of what character we cannot be certain) that beckoned them over into Mace.

[1] *The Guiding Hand of God*, Rendel Harris, p. 43- (N.C.E.F.C.)

donia and carried with it the assurance of a divine commission. And when they left Troas for Neapolis, they left Asia for Europe, and we begin to see a purpose in a course that must have been most perplexing to Paul. He couldn't know, and no man alive could know, that the centre of the world's life was going to move still further West and North, and that a group of unimportant islands barely on the fringe of civilisation and known only for tin, would share in the European domination and become at last the commercial and colonising centre of the world. But it was so, and looking back over history we feel that this journey of Paul's was fraught with the utmost significance for the Gospel, for he was being led, in the face of his own reasoned conclusions, in those directions and to those centres where his work was to have the most enduring consequences. In the very nature of the case, guidance must sometimes be obeyed without reason. Sometimes the reason becomes clear as one goes. Sometimes it doesn't. But the disciple who is living close to God, studying His word and keeping within the Christian fellowship, will be safeguarded from the dangers to which this willing obedience appears to expose him.

One other group of questions demands an answer. People sometimes ask, " Suppose you were guided to put your head into a gas oven, or to run off with another man's wife, or to steal somebody's purse, or . . . ?" There is no end to their bright imaginings.

It is difficult to know in what spirit to deal with such questions. Perhaps Proverbs xxvi. 5 gives us the best cue, though the serious answer is, of course, that we are simply not guided to any of those things. Nor should that surprise the intelligent. God's will is not in question in any of those matters, nor indeed in thousands of others. Guidance leads us sometimes to the audacious but never to the sinful.

Anything can be caricatured. The Anti-God society makes caricatures of the crucifixion. And it amuses some people to collect, and invent, fantastic tales to illustrate the folly of the Group Movement and the vagaries of " guidance." Nor need we deny that, here and there, we have known the word used as a cover for conceit and sometimes definitely misapplied by novices. But the citation of these infrequent instances is no sufficient answer to the opportunity.

Let any man ask himself which is the more dangerous life : to live by the devices of his own unaided reason, or to reason in the light of God ? Let him ask also if he has any right to deny the reality of guidance, even when it outruns the reach of rational approbation until, in patient earnestness, he has sought to prove it for himself. Then he will surely say with a new meaning,

" Guide *me*, O Thou great Jehovah."

CHAPTER VII

THROUGH THE BIBLE

Thy word is a lamp unto my feet, and a light unto my path.—THE PSALMIST.

Search the scriptures; for in them ye think ye have eternal life : and they are they which testify of me.—JESUS.

IN September 1931, the divers of the famous salvage ship *Artiglio* entered on the penultimate phase of their task on the sunken *Egypt*. They were in quest of gold. Through successive seasons the treasure-ship had been sought, located, marked and surveyed, and now the time had come to cut away that section of the main deck which formed the roof of the bullion room. A good deal of debris had collected on the spot, consisting in large part of refuse from the pantry and kitchen, and forming a mass of very smelly black mud. And, as the gold-seekers began to clear it away, a strange object came to light. It looked like part of an old book : rats had gnawed its edges : the restless waters of the Bay of Biscay had rolled over it for years : it was coated in slime and unpleasant to handle. But when it had been washed and dried, a printed page appeared, and those who could read English on board the *Artiglio* knew what they had found. It was part of a Bible. The story of David and Jonathan lay before them in black and white. They had begun to find treasure and their first discovery was a fragment of the book of God.

Now, that is a parable. Again and again, in the passage of time, men have supposed that the Bible had outlived its usefulness and need no longer be reckoned

with. In the early centuries it was often criticised for
its lack of literary style. Augustine, prior to his conversion, felt that the Scriptures were " unworthy to be
compared with the dignity of Tully." In later years,
science was said to have entirely discredited the book.
Voltaire thought that nobody would be reading the Bible
in the nineteenth century, but, in the twentieth, the demand for it is greater than ever. The seventy years of
specially keen and scholarly criticism through which the
book has just passed was a fiercer ordeal than any other
book has ever been subjected to. But it has stood the
test. Some positions have been abandoned by the
great majority of scholars, but the Bible stands authenti-
cated as the very Book of God. All the more important
epistles of Paul are accepted as being definitely his. It is
not seriously questioned that Mark's Gospel belongs to
the third quarter of the first century, and Matthew and
Luke not very much later, while the Old Testament has
become, by reason of this ordeal, an intelligible and
precious book to many people for the first time. And,
all the while, God has been guiding the faithful through
the medium of this book, teaching them great lessons
concerning Himself, concerning their fellow-men, and
leading them also in the details of their own daily life.
In prayer we speak to God. The Bible is one great
way in which God speaks to us. None who seeks
guidance can afford to neglect the Book. Let us consider how God guides through the Bible.

Some devout people have substitutes for the Scriptures.
They find the Bible a somewhat bewildering library, so
they live on little books of " selections " or even on
" promise boxes." We will not say that these aids are
without any value at all, but we are certain that they are
no sufficient substitute for the Bible. This is not to say
that all parts of the Scriptures are equally helpful We do
not think that they are. The Song of Solomon is not as
precious as the Gospel of John, but selections from the
Scriptures would have to be made very skilfully to do

justice to the infinite variety of revelation. As to the
" promise box," it will do as a sweetmeat but it must not
be made into the whole meal. It is all comfort. If one
doesn't read " My Grace is sufficient for thee," it is " No
good thing will He withhold from them that walk
uprightly," or " I will uphold thee with the right hand
of My righteousness," or "I will never leave thee nor
forsake thee." But God has other things for us beside
comfort. J. H. Newman said, in the year of his ordina-
tion, " Those who make comfort the great subject of their
preaching seem to mistake the end of their ministry.
Holiness is the great end." God gives us comfort when
we need it, but we have need also for counsel as well as
comfort, and for reproof and restraint. That is why the
" promise box " and similar selections are no sufficient
substitute for the Bible. . . . Take the *Bible*. Let God
speak to you through His own Book.

But in urging you to take the Bible, we do not suggest
that it be treated as a book of magic. It is our privilege
and duty to *study* it. The practice of opening the book
at random and receiving the first word one reads as a
personal divine message has been fruitful of much harm.
We will not say that God has *never* responded to such
methods. He treats the spiritual babe as a babe, and
sometimes answers the importunity of the mature by such
a means. John Wesley made occasional use of the
Scriptures in this way, generally when his mind was overwrought, though it was never a substitute with him for
the close daily study of the Book. On the morning of
May 24, 1738, he opened the Testament on these words,
" Thou art not far from the Kingdom of God," and at a
quarter to nine the same evening the great experience
came.

But all this must be treated as exceptional. God
cannot desire that the only use we make of His Book is
to treat it, in moments of crisis, like a lucky dip. We
must *study* the Bible. Obviously, so far as the Book is
concerned, God can guide most those who study it most.

How, then, shall we study the Bible to get the maximum guidance from its page?

We shall study it first with *prayer*. As we take it in hand, let us recollect ourselves in the presence of God. The Book has been written by men specially guided by the Holy Spirit, and it will only be understood, in all its richness, by those who have the same divine help.

We shall study it every day—and *unhurriedly*. However little time we have at our disposal, let our study of the Book be without haste. There can be little value in a chapter hurriedly scanned and the mind diverted, at once, to something else. Take less. A chapter is often too much. It is commonly allowed that when one begins the study of a fresh book of the Bible, it should be read right through first and, if possible, at a sitting, in order to get a general idea of the ground that is covered. But when one comes to its closer study, it should be taken paragraph by paragraph and, possibly, sentence by sentence. Don't make a fetish of finishing a chapter. The deeper you get into it, the less you will need. F. W. Faber said that one commonplace truth, which would seem tame and trivial to the beginner, suffices a saint for hours. The study of some books, especially in the Old Testament, requires something in the way of expert introduction if one is really to understand the historical background and see the purpose of the book in the life of the times. If possible, seek this expert help and do not begrudge the patient labour its understanding will demand; but if, for any good reason, this is not possible, do not assume that the book is closed to you because of that. Certainly, you will miss something, but not necessarily the more important thing.

Because, of course, when we turn to a portion of Scripture and quietly seek its meaning, not carrying our preconceived ideas to it but just keeping an open mind to what it has to teach, we ask two questions. " What did it mean then? " " What does it mean for me now? " Sometimes the two answers will coincide.

Sometimes the answer to the first question will elude us and yet the passage can still have personal worth. Sometimes the answer to the first question is quite clear, but it may be outside the area of our need to-day.

As instances of complete correspondence in meaning, one thinks of the ten commandments and the basic moral teaching of the Bible. When we compare the imprecatory psalms with the words of Jesus, we see at once that the principle of development in morals has its place in the Scriptures, but the impressive fact about the early Hebrews is not that they sometimes shared the primitive morality of the period, but that they so often soared above it. The ten commandments are still the basis of all advanced moral teaching. The passage of time has not discredited them. Civilised communities may not be in danger of making graven images of the kind that the second commandment condemns, but the insensate quest for money and " things " rather than for a quality of life makes the commandment meaningful even to-day.

And what is true of the second commandment is true also of so much else in Scripture. Its original meaning may no longer be pertinent, but it still has point in our personal life. The story of Abraham's sacrifice of Isaac may seem to some as nothing but an old tale, having no meaning now. But to the student of morals it marks the nation's realisation that God did not require human sacrifice, and to the simple disciple, in search of his daily help from the Book of God, it puts a new stress on the need of surrender. God's guidance through the Bible is not limited to the repetition of exact circumstances. These vary with every age. But His quest for true worshippers (John iv. 23) spans the centuries, and those who would respond to Him in these latter days learn most of His nature and will from the record of His dealing with men in time past. Nobody can read the Bible devoutly and not learn much about God, and himself, and his fellows. Nobody who seriously seeks divine guidance can neglect this most rich and sure way to it.

Many are the systems of daily reading which the Bible student may use, and most of them are commendably made. But if the student prefers to work on his own it will help him to know that common experience goes to prove that a start would be more profitably made with the Gospels than with Genesis. The most-read part of the Old Testament is the Book of Psalms. Early attention should be given, in the New Testament, to the Pauline epistles read in conjunction with Acts, and, in the Old Testament, to the Prophets.[1]

And a rich reward awaits him. As he questions the Scriptures, devoutly asking in the felt-presence of God, " What can I learn about God from this ? " " What can I learn about myself ? " " Does this Scripture rebuke me or challenge me ? " " Does it call for action, or confession, or restitution ? "—as he questions the record, the Divine Spirit will answer him and God will speak to his need. Often in the press of daily life, and in the hour of swift temptation, words of Scripture will leap up from his memory and speak themselves in his soul with the authority of Sinai. Old words take on new meanings. Familiar words shine with a fresh light. General statements press home a personal application. So God guides. For it is never enough to say that God has *spoken* through the Scriptures. God *speaks* through them still.

[1] Cf. *How to Enjoy the Bible*, A. C. Deane. (Hodder and Stoughton.)

CHAPTER VIII

THROUGH THE FELLOWSHIP

> Only in the religious atmosphere and in supreme love to God can be found the deepest and most enduring friendship among men.—PELOUBET.

Every human eye has a blind spot. It is situated at the entrance of the optic nerve and is insensible to light and colour. Many men have pleaded, in explanation of an accident, that the object had fallen upon their blind spot and they hadn't seen it.

It is no uncommon thing for men to have a blind spot upon their spiritual eye; sometimes it is a blind *patch*. They indulge themselves in some sin, or harbour and husband a weakness of the soul, and honestly cannot see the peril they are in. Prophet Harris, of French West African fame, was a good man and, in some ways, a great one. But he was a polygamist. Dr. Joseph Parker seems never to have recognised his egoism as a sin. Thomas Shillitoe, the bold Quaker missionary, was both impetuous and irritable. Nor is it fair to speak with easy scorn of such men and suggest that they saw their sin with wide eyes and were wanton. They were men of prayer. In the service of God they displayed a zeal above their fellows and their names will live for centuries in the history of the Church. Their sin was on the blind spot. What was patent to everybody else was hid from them or but dimly seen.

Now that is one of the great gains of intimate Christian fellowship. The things we cannot see ourselves, but others see so plainly in us, can be pointed out and put right. Unlike the blind spot on our natural eye, this defect in our spiritual vision can be definitely cured.

A solitary Christian is almost a contradiction in terms. Circumstances sometimes force a disciple to live a lonely life, but the loss he suffers is not a loss merely in his feelings. If his loneliness is prolonged he will lose in all ways. His vital growth depends upon sharing and service, as well as upon prayer and meditation. More than this. God's guidance, in its completeness and corroboration, requires the fellowship as well.

It is not difficult to see why. Quite reverently we can say that God's task in building anyone's character is made easier by every surrendered member of the group. God has as many avenues of approach to the heart of a man or woman, as they have friends who are friends of Christ. We bear our glad witness to the fact that God speaks to us constantly without any intermediary at all— but we bear witness also to our need of His voice through the fellowship. The sins we are strangely blind to, He can show us by a friend. The tasks He is pressing on us but which, by reason of sloth or modesty or dullness of understanding, we are leaving undone, He can call us to through the group. The doubts which fill the mind at times when our personal guidance is not clear, can be resolved in the fellowship and our path confirmed or corrected by the common mind. Let us look at some of the ways in which God guides us through the group.

The writer has a friend, a devout Christian, who was an indulgent father. He was steadily spoiling his children by giving them too much of their own way. All his friends could see his folly. He was utterly blind to it himself.

He is in no sense a weak character; definitely the reverse. In all the business relationships of life he is exact and methodical, and well aware that while business demands just dealing, it leaves little margin for generosity. Nobody knowing him outside the home would regard him as easy-going and irresolute. Perhaps that was the very reason why he couldn't see his own fault. This habit of careless indulgence was no flaw running through his character as a whole; it was confined to the hearth-side. Constant firmness in all his business dealings fashioned the thought in his mind that he was always a firm man. And everybody must relax sometimes. So he relaxed at home.

He kept his quiet time. He waited on God in the silence and felt reproved for other faults—but not this—though God, as he now believes, was thrusting it on his notice again and again. Finally, God spoke to him through two friends. Both of them were led, privately, but almost at the same time, to point out the same fault in identical words. They said, " You are an Eli." And when he went into the quietness with this stunning statement in his ears, God confirmed it, definitely, completely, leaving no element of doubt. So the blind spot was cured and he sought God's help to correct his error and " his whole body was full of light."

Many men have faults that are patent to their friends but hidden from themselves. These faults are sometimes the subject of familiar jokes. Everybody laughs at the latest illustration because everybody sees the point at once. Smith's vanity. Jones' pessimism. Robinson's meanness. Everybody knows—but nobody tells him, even though they may be attending the same Church and kneeling together at Communion. It wouldn't do to *tell* him. He might take umbrage. One would need a special atmosphere and a degree of *spiritual* intimacy before one could say that. So he walks along the path of life with his blind spot, and sometimes when his back is turned there's a general laugh.

It is not claiming a whit too much for a vital fellowship to say that it provides all the spiritual intimacy that is necessary for this frank dealing with one another, and many can tell how God has convicted them through the private word of a loving friend.

But the service of the group is not confined only to the pointing out of faults. God calls us often to *fuller service* by His voice through the fellowship. Here is a

C

girl whose timid, shrinking nature is taking on an astonishing robustness since she surrendered to Christ. All her life she has been shy. Indeed, it was the stigmatising of shyness as a sin that first made her vocal in the fellowship, and led her to a timid protest against calling a temperamental weakness a sin. But she calls it a sin herself now. She sees that it was a barrier between herself and other people, and prevented God using her. Yet, even after her great experience the bias of her nature is to doubt the call of God in her own soul. She feels unworthy. " Surely God has somebody better fitted for the task than I," she says. " He cannot want *me* to do this . . . or that." So God calls her through the fellowship and stresses the commission, already in her heart, by His word on the lips of others and, convinced by such confirmations, her hesitations end and she goes gladly to do His will.

Or, perhaps, the disciple is hesitating at a difficult interview, or growing lax with his period of daily devotion, or slipping down from his new level of life to the ineffective routine of conventional Christianity. The fellowship holds him up and keeps the challenge high. Every week brings its time of refreshment and God fulfils His promise made to the twos and threes. He is in the midst to guide; from self to surrender; from sin to holiness; from sloth to service; from the vision seen in a glass darkly to those blinding moments when we dare to say we see Him face to face. Robert Barclay knew the secret. He said, " When I came into the silent assemblies of God's people, I felt a secret power among them which touched my heart; and, as I gave way unto it, I found the evil weakening in me and the good raised up."

Nor does the service of the fellowship end even here. One of the commonest fears felt about simple faith in divine guidance is that it will lead to unchecked individualism. That the danger is a real one it is impossible to deny. The claim to an authoritative voice in the soul is a claim for which we most earnestly contend, but we are not blind to the peril of it. It is made at the first in a wondering whisper, but men sometimes slip into a loose use, and over-use, of the term and bawl about it in a way that would make a saint shudder. So often, too, men take the word with them when they cross the line that separates the path of duty from the path of mere desire and prate about guidance to bolster an argument. Is there no safeguard from all this?

The group is the safeguard. No company of Christians has had more experience both of the preciousness and the peril of this teaching than the Quakers, and in the *Friends' Book of Discipline* it says:

> "Inward guidance does not mean unchecked individualism, for the follower of the light will be continually correcting his first perception of it by a fuller experience, and by that of others who have followed it more faithfully." [1]

Not all guidance requires the confirmation of the group. Much that God says to His listening servant concerns his own personal and intimate life and provokes no question of truth or authority. But in the service of the immature, and when the voice in one's soul is not clear (an experience known to the most seasoned of God's servants) the guidance of the group is invaluable. Extravagances are corrected, hesitations removed or confirmed, and the experience of all is made mobile by God's Spirit in the service of each.

In the eager rush of early discipleship one is exposed to all kinds of dangers. Impetuousness, for instance. Nothing daunts one's dancing heart. No sacrifice seems too big. Indeed, the bigger the better. It is stiff work to learn that *obedience* is better than sacrifice. But God can teach us through the group.

[1] *Christian Life, Faith and Thought*, p. 84. (Friends' Bookshop.)

When God is weaning one's soul from mere feeling, and teaching His growing child to count less and less on emotional raptures, it is hard to be sure always that the guidance is definitely His. "But I don't *feel* any great thrill at the thought of it," we say. Does that matter? Confirmed in the fellowship we arise to do His bidding, counting it sufficient reward to be trusted, and conscious of having grown beyond the stage when every errand earned a sweet.

It cannot be denied that where the general level of experience in the fellowship is immature, its ability to check the guidance of its members is definitely limited. But that is a practical difficulty which will not often arise. The very survival of these cells of vital spiritual life depends, under God, on leadership that is mature, as well as consecrated, and the confirmation, or correction, of the group will show all the marks of sanctified common sense. Panelled into the rich background of the Church's wider life, and drawing thence its lessons of past mistakes and dangers, the groups will increase in ability to check the guidance of individual members, and help them to distinguish the voice of God from the murmurs of vanity and self-will.

PERPLEXED, BUT NOT IN DESPAIR

CHAPTER IX

IS IT ALL TOO TRIVIAL?

Are not five sparrows sold for two farthings, and not one of them is forgotten before God? But even the very hairs of your head are all numbered.

. . . ye are of more value than many sparrows.—JESUS.

You say, " You allow a *general* Providence, but deny a *particular* one." What is a general, of whatever kind it be, that includes no particulars? Is not every general necessarily made up of its several particulars? Tell me any genus, if you can, that contains no species? What is it that constitutes a genus but so many species added together? What is a whole that contains no parts? Mere nonsense and contradiction!—JOHN WESLEY.

O<small>NE</small> of the commonest objections that is made to a belief in the detailed guidance of God concerns what the critics call the triviality of the things " communicated." That God guides in the big issues of life, many of them will allow; but when it comes to writing a certain letter or catching a particular train . . . the thing is too foolish for words. We have already dealt with what seems to us the basic fallacy of this objection but we have not yet given a complete reply. Two other aspects of the matter might well be considered here.

First, *what is a trivial thing?* The word " trivial " and all its synonyms are really relative terms. They imply a comparison. Nothing is simply " small." It is small in reference to something else and, if the standard of comparison is changed, it may be large. Ben Nevis, for instance, as compared with the Alps or the Himalayas, is an unnoticeable bump, but within the British Isles it is a considerable peak, the mightiest mountain of all. We have merely changed the standard of measurement. The Thames besides the Amazon or the Orinoco is a rivulet, a babbling brook, a tiny trickle, but compared with the other rivers of these islands it is a long and noble stream. " Small " is a relative term. When people are disposed to wave a thing aside as being " too trivial " to be guidance, one is impelled to ask, " Too trivial in comparison with *what* ? "

A broken toy is a real tragedy to a child. It can be replaced for a couple of shillings, but the child sobs his heart out, and it is callous to be impatient with his grief. As Francis Thompson says in his essay on Shelley :

" Children's griefs are little, certainly; but so is the child, so is its endurance, so is its field of vision, while its nervous impressionability is keener than ours. Grief is a matter of relativity; the sorrow should be estimated by its proportion to the sorrower; a gash is as painful to one as an amputation to another. Pour a puddle into a thimble or an Atlantic into Etna; both thimble and mountain overflow. Adult fools ! would not the angels smile at *our* griefs, were not angels too wise to smile at them ? " [1]

Our griefs? People who claim a special power to discern the importance of things and wave aside something of significance in another life because it seems to them to be trivial, must be careful. They may prove more than they wish. The death of your dearest is a triviality to one who thinks cosmically. What significance can it have in the movement of the ages ? But if faith can cry for comfort in such an hour—and find it—then faith has grasped the truth of God's Fatherhood, and if God is our Father, His care will run down to details. No father treats a thing as unimportant that

[1] *Works of Francis Thompson*, Vol. III, p. 10. (Burns, Oates and Washbourne, Ltd.)

is of real concern to his child. He will spend an hour in mending an old toy if, at the same time, he soothes a torn heart.

Or look at it in terms of money. Sixpence is a trivial coin to a wealthy man. However much he may have laid to heart the maxim that, if one looks after the pennies the pounds will look after themselves, he cannot seriously consider sixpence. A copy of *Punch*, a tip to a porter, the price of a shave. What is sixpence?

A great deal if one is very poor. George Gissing knew the value of sixpence. He had been poor himself and in *The Private Papers of Henry Ryecroft* he makes us feel the tragedy of a lost sixpence in a poor home.

" Near a hamlet in a lonely spot by a woodside, I came upon a little lad of perhaps ten years old who, his head hidden in his arms against a tree-trunk, was crying bitterly. I asked him what was the matter, and after a little trouble . . . I learnt that, having been sent with sixpence to pay a debt, he had lost the money. The poor little fellow was in a state of mind which, in a grown man, would be called the anguish of despair; he must have been crying for a long time; every muscle in his face quivered as if under torture; his limbs shook, his eyes, his voice uttered such misery as only the vilest criminal should be made to suffer. And it was because he had lost sixpence!! I could have shed tears with him, tears of pity and of rage at all this spectacle implied. On a day of indescribable glory, when earth and heaven shed benediction upon the soul of man, a child whose nature would have bidden him rejoice, as only childhood may, wept his heart out because his hand had dropped a sixpenny-piece. The loss was a very serious one and he knew it; he was less afraid to face his parents than overcome by misery at the thought of the harm that he had done them. Sixpence dropped by the wayside and a whole family made wretched!

What are the due descriptive terms for a state of 'civilisation' in which such a thing as this is possible? I put my hand in my pocket and wrought sixpenny-worth of miracle." [1]

It is all comparative. Let us hesitate to stigmatise anything as trivial. Samuel Chadwick used to say that the most important thing he ever did in his life was to clean a pair of boots. It registered his decision for Jesus and expressed his adoption of a fixed principle to do everything as unto, and for, his Lord. If a straw can show the direction of the wind, a simple act of obedience can show the consecration of a whole life. Quite clearly, it isn't easy to say what is a trivial thing.

Secondly, it is clear to any keen observer of life that *big events turn on apparent trivialities*. Heavy doors, we have been reminded, swing on small hinges. The door of the London Safe Deposit, in Lower Regent Street, London, weighs twenty tons. Compared to the door, the hinges are insignificant. But it turns on them and would be utterly useless without them.

The most important events in human life often turn on little things. Dr. J. H. Jowett intended, as a young man, to go into the legal profession. Indeed, all the arrangements were made for him to enter a Halifax firm of solicitors as an articled clerk, but, on the day before the articles were to be signed, he met, by accident in the street, his old Sunday School teacher and told him what he was about to do. Mr. Dewhirst looked his disappointment. "I had always hoped," he said, "that you would go into the ministry." Jowett went home deep in thought. Looking into his own heart he found a definite inclination towards the ministry, but he questioned himself anxiously as to whether it was a Divine call. He was standing by the harmonium in the parlour. As he waited, the call came. He calls it "a grip," a "gracious constraint," and from that moment

[1] *The Private Papers of Henry Ryecroft*, George Gissing, pp. 8 f.

he had no hesitation. The articles were never signed and a few weeks later he had been accepted at Airedale College as a candidate for the ministry.

What a little thing! A " chance " meeting with a good man in the street, but surely God was in it, for He called a prince to His pulpit that day and directed a soul whose preaching and writing blessed the lives of thousands—among whom the Archbishop of Canterbury was glad to number himself.

Or take the case of Dr. Albert Schweitzer. In the Whitsuntide holidays of 1896, he made up his mind that he would devote himself to art and science until he was thirty, and afterwards to the direct service of humanity. The words of Jesus wrought this decision in his mind. " Whosoever would save his life shall lose it; and whosoever shall lose his life for my sake and the Gospel's shall save it."

But the quest for a sphere of service did not prove easy. He thought first of caring for, and educating, abandoned children, and then winning a pledge from them, as they grew up, to serve similar children in the same way. But his efforts to find such work always proved unsuccessful. His thought turned next to tramps and discharged prisoners and for a while he assisted in work among these men. But no conviction of having found his real sphere came with any of these tasks, and that he was finally led to it, Schweitzer says, " I have always regarded as a signal instance of the mercy which has again and again been vouchsafed to me."

It happened like this. One evening, in the autumn of 1904, he found one of the green-covered magazines of the Paris Missionary Society on his desk in the college and, in the very act of putting it aside to get on with his work, he opened it mechanically and caught sight of an article headed, " The Needs of the Congo Mission."

" It was by Alfred Boegner, the President of the Paris Missionary Society, an Alsatian, and contained a complaint that the Mission had not enough workers to carry on its work in the Gaboon, the northern province of the Congo Colony. The writer expressed his hope that the appeal would bring some of those ' on whom the Master's eyes already rested ' to a decision to offer themselves for this urgent work. The conclusion ran : ' Men and women who can reply simply to the Master's call, " Lord, I am coming," these are the people whom the Church needs.' The article finished, I quietly began my work. My search was over." [1]

So all the glorious work at Lambaréné turned on so trivial a thing as a green-covered magazine and its " mechanical " opening. That Schweitzer would have found a sphere of useful service in any case cannot be doubted. But it cannot be doubted either that a " little " thing directed him to the disease-ridden swamps of Equatorial Africa or that God has been able to do a Christlike work with him in Gaboon. Quite clearly, the most consequential things in life often turn on trivialities.

But let us leave the rôle of defenders for a moment and put a question to the critics. Can the people who claim to see, from the degree of its importance, whether a thing is likely to be guidance or not, tell us, in contrast to these trivialities, what is a *really* important thing ? We have put this question a few times but the answer has never seemed quite satisfactory. " A big business deal," one friend suggested. A big business deal ! Well, it *may* be important. Much reflection on these matters has made us less bold than some people to state categorically what is important and what is not. But, quite frankly, it does not seem a bit *obvious* to us that a contract secured by one firm and lost by another is ultimately more important than that Samuel Chadwick should clean those boots and express a life-consecration

[1] Albert Schweitzer : *My Life and Thought*, p. 107. (George Allen and Unwin, Ltd.)

in so doing. If character is the sterling of eternity, then all " big business " is merely an occasion for meeting people, and the *purpose* and *value* of meeting may have very little to do with the business itself. Look at it in the light of eternity. One of the greatest business deals in the history of the world was the diamond amalgamation of South Africa. Four men met to debate it. Cecil Rhodes and Beit on one side. Woolf Joel and Barnato on the other. It was " a game played in millions " and the oldest of the players was only thirty-five.

And was all that an obviously more important thing than the strange " chance " by which David Livingstone, a lad of twenty, came to read an appeal by Mr. Gutzlaff to the Churches of Britain and America on behalf of China, and was led at the last to the heart of Africa, an apostle of love to the Negro people ?

We meet and do business, we sell and buy goods, but all the time the most important thing is the influence of our characters on one another and the development within us of that quality of life which endures. A big business deal may be a thing of great importance, but it will not be greatly important simply because it is big business, but because of some other element in it which may be found just as certainly in what seems to be a triviality.

What is a *really* important thing—obviously and ultimately important and of such a character that it denies denial ? It is not easy to say, because the very question involves an appeal to some kind of standard and the answer will depend upon the character of that appeal. Even the things that most excited our pride in humanity and seemed undeniably important, have sometimes disappointed us. The aeroplane, for instance. Lord Trenchard, having spent the best years of his life perfecting the art of flying, wishes, most earnestly, that it had never been invented, for there is admittedly no protection from the aerial bomber. One thing is clear.

It is plainly not possible to decide by some rough assessment of its importance, whether a thing is guided or not. The unwilling visit of a little man to a room in Aldersgate Street was far more consequential for the world than many Acts of Parliament, and the fabric of our human life is so strangely woven that we may well hesitate to deny the hand of the Divine Weaver because the witness of our neighbour seems so small.

CHAPTER X

WHAT IF CALAMITY COMES ?

He guideth me . . . though I walk through the valley
of the shadow. . . .—DAVID.

Let us look up to the work of Jesus in the plan and arrange-
ment of our lives, and believe that He is doing His very best
for us. We may not always like the way by which we are
being led, but let us silence objection and complaint by the
deliberate choice of the will to be led by Him come what may.
The flesh may sometimes shrink, as His did in Gethsemane;
nevertheless, let the will hold its course right onward, daring
to trust its Leader, daring to believe that He knows the best
path and is taking it, daring to perform what He appoints
and bear what He imposes or permits, in complete indifference
to the voices that bid us spare ourselves.—F. B. MEYER.

Not everything happens
in the world just as God wishes. When people say,
" Whatever is, is best," they cannot really mean what
they say, or they mean it with certain conditions and
reservations which filch the literal meaning from the
words. If, in simple truth, " Whatever is, is best,"
then this is paradise and, as Leibnitz argued, the best of
all possible worlds.

But we find that hard to believe, even when we give
the closest heed to the German philosopher's reasoning
and allow that " a little bitter is often more pleasing
than sugar." Is evil merely a privation, a deficiency, a
limitation ?—the shading of the picture or the discord
in the music, just added to heighten and enhance the
effect ? Can we say with Browning " the evil is null,
is naught, is silence implying sound " ?

Voltaire makes merry over Leibnitz' reasoning and

79

gives it as his opinion that this is the *worst* of all possible worlds, and while we shrink back from that absurd caricature, we cannot feel that this is " paradise enow." Sin seems too positive. Evil leaves its slimy trail over so much that might be fair and beautiful. We pray, " Thy will be done on earth, as it is in heaven," because, as yet, the correspondence of earth and heaven is far from complete.

The writer met a friend one day, a minister, returning from a funeral. Even allowing for the sad errand which had occupied his mind, he seemed peculiarly low-spirited. " I have just buried a child," he said, " and the child's father is under arrest for manslaughter. Last Saturday evening, it seems, he came home drunk, clambered into the bed where his wife and the little one were asleep and in his fuddled condition pushed the baby out of bed. It fell and, as it fell, the child's head struck the fender. In the grey light of the next morning they found the little body cold and dead upon the floor. The police were called, of course, and the father is in prison awaiting his trial.

" But that wasn't the whole of it," my friend went on. " After the interment, one of the mourners, trying to make a little pious talk in the parson's presence, said, ' Ah well! It can't be helped, I suppose. It was the will of God.'

" The will of God ? " said my friend bitterly. " That wasn't the will of God. God could never have wished that that dear child be pushed to death by a drunken brute. It was a horrible travesty of all that God would have wished for the little one."

As we parted, I turned the old problem over in my mind again. What happens to the guidance of God when calamity comes ? Calamity isn't always the outcome of obvious sin. It overtakes the saints. Untimely death has nipped the life of the noblest souls, and not death merely, but death through agonising pain. Thomas Arnold, the great headmaster, the friend of God and of boyhood, struck down at forty-seven with angina pectoris. F. W. Robertson, fearless thinker and friend of the working man, passed out at thirty-seven with a terrible abscess in the cerebellum. Henry Drummond, whom Ian Maclaren called "the most perfect Christian I have known or expect to see this side of the grave," died at the age of forty-six after two years on his back in pain. Nor is that the problem at its worst. Hardly a year passes but some great disaster stuns the public mind. The Tay Bridge disaster. The ramming of the *Victoria*. The loss of the *Titanic*. The wreck of the R *101*. No easy answer leaps to our lips. The man who finds in all such disasters the judgment of God on a wicked people is both unconvincing and inhuman. Choice souls perish in such an hour, and these calamities visit a thrifty and industrious people as well as a profligate and frivolous one. Disaster, like the rain, falls on the just and the unjust. The horror of it strikes one dumb, and when speech returns, a tempest of questions rises to the lips. *Does* God guide us? Is there knowledge in the Most High? Does He lead us to the lip of a calamity and leave us to fall in? The problem demands an attempt at an answer because any day might thrust it on our notice again and because it challenges faith. If anguish comes, can doubt be far behind?

It is the opinion of the writer that the perfect will of God is constantly thwarted by human ignorance, stupidity, carelessness and sin. No other view seems tenable as one looks at this chaotic world. It is a consequence of God's great gift to men of freedom, and without that freedom we should be marionettes and not men. We are born, moreover, into a society and a world where the perfect will of God has been thwarted for ages, and we are bound up in the bundle of life with our fellows. We gain immeasurably by these relationships. We can love one another, serve, help and influence one another; necessarily we can also harm one another as well. We could not have the blessing without the risk of the bane.

God took the risk. Everything sweet in this life has come to us from others. Our mothers suffered pain to give us birth. Our fathers worked for us. When we were ill, doctors and nurses bent their strength and skill to make us better, and our dear ones turned night into day as they watched at our side. Nor were we allowed to grow up untutored in mind or soul. We were educated. All that clever men and women had ever discovered, or thought, was put before us in ways we could take in, and the best the world has ever learned in things spiritual was made attractive too. We learned the name of Jesus. The imperishable stories of the Bible were told us, and all along the path of life precious things, the *most* precious, have come to us from other people. Friendship, counsel, encouragement, love—streaming in on us from others because God has set us here in a great family life, and made us so that our lives intertwine. It should not surprise us, in the light of all we gain, that there is some risk of loss as well. When God made us so that we could love and help one another, He exposed His family to the possibility that they would hate and harm one another. Necessarily. The one goes with the other. And sin came in, with its long entail of sorrow and suffering, and we can be hurt at any time by the folly, carelessness or crime of another. But would you rather live in a world in which that couldn't happen? Do you wish God had so made us that we could never influence each other, never be friends, never guide, comfort or help each other . . . never *love*? It would be a hateful and unendurable existence, loathsome to us all.

God's will, we believe, for His children, is the perfection of their characters and their ultimate bliss, but the cast of our inherited nature and the conditions of a sin-spoilt world do not allow an easy path to that great end. God therefore permits the woes of life to press upon us; the consequences of our own sin and sometimes the sin of others; the consequences of our carelessness and ignorance, and the carelessness and ignorance of others. The loss of the *Titanic* was due to reckless racing through an ice-field, and the death-roll was lengthened by the fact that she only carried boat accommodation for 1,200 people, though the passengers and crew totalled 2,293. It was a compound of pride and criminal folly. But W. T. Stead was among the passengers, going to America in the interests of world peace and to take part in the " Men and Religion Forward Movement." He was drowned.

Yet God meets us in every situation, hears the cry which our bleeding hearts fling to Him, and bears with us when, in bitterness, we question His restraint, deny His love, and doubt His existence. Granted a willing and responsive heart in us, He can so turn tragedy to triumph, and loss to gain, that men have even believed that *He* sent the pain and devised the disaster, so marvellously does He bring good out of evil. Think how closely joy and pain are interwoven in the fabric of our human lives. Our achievements in love *measure* our capacity for pain. Before I knew my friend or cared for him, his doings were of no account to me. He could pass me in the street with a frozen stare, I did not mind. He did not sympathise with me in my trouble, and I did not miss his sympathy. When success came to me, he sent no congratulations, but it did not make me grave. We were outside each other's circle and we had no sense of lack. But when I learned to love my friend, I armed him with the power to wound me deeply. I put a weapon in his hand and exposed my heart to its bare point. The more I loved, the more he could wound. If he ignores me now, I am hurt. If he denies his sympathy, I miss it. If he lapses into sin, I share the shame. Love has made me vulnerable, it has exposed me to pain, because pain and love are inextricably interwoven in the only kind of life we know.

If sin had never spoilt this fair earth . . . if men had

always done the perfect will of God . . . if our poor race had responded at every stage to the leading of the loving Father . . . anything might have happened then. Perhaps there would have been no need of sympathy in such a world. Perhaps character would have grown without discipline. Perhaps love would never have been linked with pain. Perhaps . . . and perhaps! But in *this* world, the only world we know, love and pain are interwoven. Mysteriously they belong together. They are united at the very portals of life. There is nothing nobler and sweeter on this planet than mother-love, but it is strangely compounded, and half its quality comes from this—that a mother goes down to the gates of death for her child. Joy impregnates : pain brings forth : love is born.

None can deny that the trouble-tossed and pain-racked people have often pioneered the way to a better world. John G. Paton, toiling for Christ beside the lonely grave of his wife and child in Tanna. Josephine Butler, bereft of her darling girl. Bishop Chavasse, the saint with a hump-back. Nor is the truth well expressed if we say that they served well in spite of their woe. They served well *because* of it. They carried it to God, and God turned it into triumph. Many a life has been saved by the loss of the *Titanic*. The track of west-bound steamers across the Atlantic was shifted further south, away from the dangerous ice-fields. The obsolete Board of Trade requirements, with regard to emergency boat accommodation, were stringently revised. Several improvements in life-saving appliances were immediately made, and wireless, which was still in the immaturity of its use, received the impetus which only tragedy can impart.

We see the gains in individual lives as well. Commenting on the sorrows that beset Dr. R. W. Dale, Robertson Nicoll says, " In him was fulfilled the great word, that the men of sorrows are the men of influence in every walk of life." Carlyle comments on the sufferings of Dante in these words : " If all had gone well with him, Florence would have had another Lord Mayor and the world would have lost the *Divina Commedia.*" Of our friends, as well as of our Saviour, we might say, " Fruitful let thy sorrows be." And not only of our friends, but of ourselves.

What, then, shall we say of guidance ? If character is His aim and not our swift enjoyment of some low way of life, should it surprise us that He does not intervene when sin or stupidity, folly or ignorance (our own or another's), brings us to the flinty pathway ? Shall we question His love because He persists in treating us as persons and not puppets, and will not rob us of our freedom to save us from our woes ? From many of these griefs and pains He could and would have saved us if we had been more sensitive to His leading, and responsive to His call, and it is the whole plea of this book that such guidance is possible, if we will but fulfil the conditions.

But in a world like ours, where we are close knit in a great family circle and our lives are constantly affected by the deeds of others, it is impossible to think that He could save us from them *all*, and when we look at our own natures in the light of God, we would hardly desire it ourselves. Disappointment, pain, grief and loss have taught us so much. Never have we walked the flinty way but we found Him on it when we called. Some of the sweetest souls we have known have walked it longer, and in far, far rougher places, but they say, " He never ceased to guide; He knew the way, knew it at its worst. A hand like this hand reached me in the darkness and led me on. Like this hand ? Like . . . and unlike ! It was rough with work at a carpenter's bench and pierced with an ancient wound."

Some are on the path with bitter hearts and lagging feet, and their lives, poor souls, are sour and unlovely. They have not found the Guide or, rather, let the Guide find them. The rebellion in their heart prevents it and the cloud never seems to lift from their toilsome way. Because they do not follow the Guide, they never reach the plains of light. They do not believe that it leads there. It does. Always, to those who will follow the Guide. It is really the path of Opportunity. Guidance does not end when calamity begins. In every situation He meets us and out of every situation He can lead us to a greener pasture and a sphere of wider use.

But when calamity has us in its grip, even this strong thought is not enough of itself. We look the ugly intruder in the face, feel its power to steal the joy from half our life, and cast our querulous inquiries at God demanding to know why it had to be. In that hour, the safeguarding of our freedom doesn't seem enough. In our bewilderment we feel that a loving God would find effective discipline some easier way. We look at Him through mists of tears and wonder if, in His greatness, He really feels our woe. Then it is that Our Lord comes and shows us His feet, His hands, His side, and if there were a tongue in every wound of Jesus, we know what it would say : " *I have suffered !* " Then it is that we feel with Emerson how nigh is grandeur to our dust, how near is God to man. He has suffered. He does not simply reign in some far-off splendour, untroubled by our woe.

> " Jesus knows *all* about our struggles.
> He will guide till the day is done."

The whole story of the Passion is rich in its power to bless. We go with Him into Gethsemane and feel, even when our own sorrow is most vivid to our thought, that we have not drunk the cup of bitterness so deep as this. In all the dark mystery of it, the shadows seem never so dark as they do in Gethsemane. The word " agony " is used of our Lord only in the Garden. He was master of Himself from the kiss of Judas till He cried with a loud voice and gave up His spirit. But in the garden . . . agony . . . the bloody sweat . . . the pleading prayer. " If it be possible, let this cup pass from me." So He prays, " first on His feet : and then on His knees : and then on His face." He knows it all : deeper, further than any of us. Beside *His* agony, our own seems to shrink. " And every cross grows light beneath the shadow, Lord, of Thine."

Then the voices through the trees and the gleaming lanterns. Judas and his leprous kiss. Poor Peter dragging the sword from beneath his garment and taking a blow at the nearest. He meant it for his head but it got only his ear. The shouts, the trampled undergrowth, the scared disciples, and the inquisitive mob.

But Jesus is master of the situation again. His will is perfectly attuned with the Father's. He is going right on by way of the Cross. Turning on Peter, He ordered the sword back into its sheath and broke their last hopes of spectacular conquest. He would not appeal to force. " Thinkest thou that I cannot beseech my Father, and He shall even now send me more than twelve legions of angels ? " But He would not call them. He was taking the long way, but the only possible way, the way of love, and no pain would turn Him back. Never had His Father broken the rule of the ages and bludgeoned His way into the unwilling hearts of men. Jesus would not ask Him to do it now. There was no discord in these wills so perfectly attuned. He would conquer sin with love. He would make the Cross a throne. He would *use* the shame and pain and humiliation of it to expose the very heart of God, and sin would not triumph : it would be but a dark background revealing, by contrast, the wonder of that love. So He takes the Cross, not of compulsion, not by mere submission or resignation, but *willingly*.

And when we see Him there, we have our greatest aid to understanding how the calamities of life can be wrested to our soul's use, and the use of others. He takes it *willingly*. His arms are not merely stretched upon it : they are wound around it. He holds it to

Him. He does not merely *suffer* it, He employs it. And so the symbol of shame becomes the focus point of glory.

In that same willing spirit He desires that we meet, and use, the calamities of life that overtake us. An evil that *can* be put right must be resisted. The call of a situation that can be corrected is not easy acquiescence but spirited opposition. But those are not the problems we are considering now. There is a finality about bereavement, an amputated limb, an incurable disease, a lost fortune. The real crosses of life have to be *borne*. Can you bear the cross willingly ? That will change it from a weight into wings : it cannot crush you : you rise by it.

> " So by my *woes* to be
> Nearer, my God, to Thee,
> Nearer to Thee ! "

Through the shadows He guides still and converts the loss into gain, working out of our folly and mistakes something which will be worthy of the price pain has paid.

Thomas Erskine of Linlathen says :

" Many things appear, and are, irretrievable to us, but there is nothing irretrievable with God. This is a great gospel to my heart. He, who knows how to take occasion from the fall to bring in the redemption, may be safely trusted with each event, and with every action, good and bad. I believe that love reigns and that love will prevail. I believe that He says to me every morning, ' Begin again thy journey and thy life; thy sins, which are many, are not only forgiven, but they shall be made, by the wisdom of God, the basis on which He will build blessings.' "

So we believe. They shall be made, by the wisdom of God, the basis on which He will build blessings. Our sins and our mistakes ! Even the saddest of our mistakes : the ones we made when we listened for His guiding voice but did not quite succeed in disentangling it from the voice of self-love. He will build a blessing on it, and in the light of heaven the mysteries will be solved, the gains of our losses made clear, and fullest scope be found for the disciplined abilities we have developed on earth.

> " Then shall I see and hear and know
> All I desired and wished below,
> And every power find sweet employ
> In that eternal world of joy."

CHAPTER XI

DOES IT DO VIOLENCE TO OUR PERSONALITY ?

God ! Thou art mind ! unto the master mind
Mind should be precious. Spare my mind alone !
All else I will endure; if as I stand
Here, with my gains, Thy thunder smite me down,
I bow me; 'tis Thy will, Thy righteous will;
I o'erpass life's restrictions, and I die;
And if no trace of my career remain
Save a thin corpse at pleasure of the wind
In these bright chambers level with the air,
See Thou to it ! But if my spirit fail,
My once proud spirit forsake me at the last,
Has Thou done well by me ?   So do not Thou !
Crush not my mind, dear God, though I be crushed !

ROBERT BROWNING.

Most students of the Scriptures are aware of the different theories of inspiration which have been held concerning the Bible. Men thought, at one time, that the Holy Spirit dictated the Scriptures to the prophets and evangelists, just as a business man dictates a letter to a typist. Various figures of speech were used to express the idea and sometimes the human agents were regarded as " pens " in the hands of the Divine Spirit, and sometimes as " harps " from which God struck the precise sound He desired. In both cases the consequence was the same. Every exact word was " given " and must be taken literally. When the Scriptures say, " And the serpent said unto the woman," we are to understand that an actual serpent spoke to her. No solecisms, it was believed, could possibly have crept into the Greek of the New Testament, and even the vowel points and accents of the Hebrew text shared the same unqualified inspiration. In its extreme forms, this theory supposed that during the act of writing the human agent was completely " controlled " and became merely a mouth for the voice of God.

While this theory is not extinct even to-day, it is not widely held. Scholars still hold to the real inspiration of the Scriptures, but they reject the suggestion that the will of God submerged the human agents and treated them as automatons. The different personalities of the writers are recognised in their work, and it is seen that the revelation of God was given to them in such measure and manner as they could understand. They did not cease to be free persons when they said with such assurance, " Thus saith the Lord." Their inspiration was not of that quality which Plato mentions in the *Timæus*.

" No man when in his wits attains prophetic truth and inspiration; but when he receives the inspired word, either his intelligence is enthralled in sleep or he is demented by some distemper or possession." [1]

The prophets and evangelists, we feel, received the inspiration of God when their spiritual insight was keenest and their intellect most active. Not by overwhelming their consciousness, but by quickening and stimulating it, did the voice of God find utterance within them.

Now, that distinction is worth bearing in mind when we consider the relationship of guidance to our personality. There are some people who speak as though God's guidance takes our consciousness by storm and " controls " us. That view has no support in these pages. Rich and manifold as are the ways by which God reveals Himself to us, and infinitely precious as they must ever be, we cannot feel that God ever *imposes*

[1] Plato, *Timæus* 71.

His will on ours, or dragoons us to His service. He respects our personality. His power never sweeps into the soul independent of our will. Even when His counsel is crystal clear in our mind, we are consciously free to accept or reject it. Though it speaks with the same imperative voice as conscience, we can be deaf with the stony deafness of those who *won't* hear.

Let us look at it in an illustration. Airmen and wireless experts are watching with keen interest the development of a " homing " wireless apparatus for aeroplanes, which is likely to be fitted in due course to all machines and affect the whole future of flying. This equipment, which is still in an immature stage, allows a pilot to tune in to any broadcasting station on his route, and, by means of a three-way switch in the cockpit, to confirm his course and travel with confidence, even though the visibility is bad and the Magnetic Pole exerting a somewhat erratic influence on his compass needle. The airman uses the usual head-receivers and, while his aeroplane is making for the transmitting station, no signals are heard, but any deviation from the true course will at once produce sounds in his ears. On receiving this warning, the pilot, by turning the switch, can discover what his position is, in relation to what it ought to be. Steering back, he can confirm it by moving the switch both to the right and to the left, and when he receives a signal of equal strength from both sides, he knows that he has found the correct course again. He is still free, if he wishes, to neglect his signals. He can ignore the warning sound and fly where the whim of the moment leads him, but he will be flying from his true path and putting himself in peril.

It is not dissimilar, we believe, with guidance. To those who, by the surrender of their life, the cultivation of the mind of Christ, and by much waiting on God, have become sensitised to His will, the path of life is made clear and they journey with a deep inner confidence. It seems like a trackless flight, but they belong to those

" whom God whispers in the ear," and they have secret communications concerning their course. They *could* ignore those communications. Neither their will nor their consciousness has been imprisoned by Omnipotence. But they say with the Psalmist, " I *delight* to do Thy will, O my God," and they find that in His will is their peace.

But the whole problem is not settled by that. Many men, who admit that this theory of guidance does not *overwhelm* our consciousness, are still of opinion that it would do violence to our personality in subtle ways. Any view of guidance which included direction by God to specific acts is felt, by some thinkers, to be untenable, because God wills us to act always on our own insight, and personality can only be achieved by the exercise of full moral freedom. If ever God does employ such detailed direction it is to be understood, these thinkers say, as a condescension to a babe in Christ, and such counsel will grow less frequent the more mature the Christian becomes.

Let us look at that criticism. There can be no doubt that if God had a plan for every detail of our life—the boot we should put on first in the morning and the bus we should catch on our journey to town—and if the plain business of each day was to obey His dictation in every detail, our moral nature would be stunted and our personality cramped. Exercise in freedom is essential to growth. It is no part of our argument that God has a precise will for every detail of every life, and " dictation " and " coercion " are not words that describe the relationship at all. But we do contend that it is possible to live so sensitive to His Will that He can counsel us, when His purpose requires it, even in details, and we cannot conceive ourselves ever growing beyond the advantage of such aid. In the keeping of twenty appointments, it may be a matter of indifference whether I go by car or train. In keeping the twenty-first appointment, it may be vitally important for my own life, or another's, that I do one and not the other.

If I am sensitive to the will of God, I will be guided which to do. The " secret hint " neither filches my consciousness nor forces my will. Neither does it rob me of the necessity for the thought and judgment by which a moral personality grows. God is pursuing sublime purposes in the world, and He can work best with those who respond most swiftly to His touch. We are dealing, not with the God of Deism, but with a Father who has numbered, says Jesus, the hairs of our head. Any conviction in a man's mind that God simply will *not* counsel him in details, insulates him from the quickening power. After all, this faith is but the heavenly counterpart of an earthly commonplace. Every father is anxious about the true development of his boy, and gives him wide scope for the exercise of judgment and decision. But he is swift also with many pointed words of counsel, which his great love and longer experience qualify him to give, but which his son's undeveloped mind may not allow him fully to understand. God's love and wisdom lie behind all His counsel of us, and vindicate it. On this earth we shall not grow beyond the need of such timely help, for our keenest vision is myopic and the tendrils of our lives intertwine with consequences that we cannot always foresee. God sees. He is leading us on to the fullest moral stature but, in the meanwhile of this earthly life, He is ready to counsel us with many a precious and personal word. Our personality cannot be harmed by such a method: it is not extravagant to expect that our moral insight will be made the keener, the more we " watch the Master work."

Another objection to this view of guidance suggests that it is " a denial of God's providence overruling all life,"

" for it tacitly assumes a conception of God which is anthropomorphic in the worst sense, namely, that which treats Him as an individual set over against His creation so that it is not the circumstances of life which are the means of His communication with His children, but rather He can impose Himself on His creation only by finding a servant, now here, now there, who is able and willing to carry out His behests in relation to certain specific occasions and events."[1]

With the larger questions provoked by this criticism we do not feel the obligation to deal, because we are not defending the extreme view which is being attacked. It is, however, of value to remember that the will of God on most difficult problems has first become clear to a servant, now here, now there, who is able and willing to carry out His behests.

No great movement ever gripped, as an immediate inspiration, the mass of mankind or even the whole Church of God. It came first to an individual, or to a tiny group, and their passion burned with white heat at the heart of the crusade they were constrained to begin. Did all England wake one morning with a burning sense of shame concerning our prison system? No! One man woke one morning with that sense of shame. God's sorrow found an echo in the heart of John Howard, who gathered about him a company of those who shared the shame, and they toiled together to bring the reformation in. One burning heart, or a passionate few, explain the human side of all great reforms. Did all England wake one morning with a burning sense of shame concerning slavery? No! A handful of evangelical Christians awoke with that sense of shame. They were opposed both within the Church and without. The Bible was quoted against them. Had not the patriarchs kept slaves? Had not Paul returned a slave to his owner? Still they went on, seeking and receiving the guidance of God. That guidance was given to them in their moral insight:

[1] *Oxford and the Groups*, p. 140.   (Blackwell.)

the deep conviction that this " sum of all the villainies "
was against the will of God.   But it was given them also,
as they believed, in guidance to specific acts and in what
seemed the " chance " making of contacts which proved
wonderfully useful to them in the prosecution of their
cause.   They marched forward, saying, " God is with
us," and they received indications of His leadership
in things small and great.

The soul is still, to some extent, an undiscovered
country, and it would be rash to assume that we understand the full extent of its working.   It may be that
there are *latent powers* in us, rudimentary at present,
but capable of rich development as we live with God
and put all our life under His sway.   The element of
mystery must be accepted, but while we wait for an
explanation, we can still witness to an experience.

One thinks, for instance, of the strange awareness
one has that the right moment has come to speak to a
person about their spiritual need and find them just
wanting that very word.   One thinks also of the almost
uncanny insight one is given of the real nature of a
person's problem when one is talking it out with them
and seeking to help.   Just as an example of the kind
of thing we mean, let us look at this second illustration
rather more closely.

Most people who have been busy in the care of souls,
and have had any length of experience in spiritual
direction, could furnish out of their own ready memory
a number of instances of this insight.

Folk come seeking help and advice, and, as they
unfold the story of their need, one is conscious that
something is being hidden and that the real heart of their
problem has not been exposed.   It may not be a deliberate deception on their part.   They may finish the
story with the relief of having made " a clean breast " of
it, but none of the usual suggestions meets their need
and clearly the peace of God passes them by.

Then it is, again and again, that, as one waits on God

in prayer and holds up the inquirers' need before Him, a conviction of their true position takes shape in one's mind. Sometimes it is a strong impression as to the *area* of their need, the segment of their life in which the trouble lies. At other times it rises in the mind with still more precision, and it is possible to put one's finger right on the spot. A few plain questions expose its very heart. Often the seeker is surprised himself, but his conscience confirms it. When, at the last, one says after further quiet talking, " It is this," he may hesitate at the cost but he does not contest the diagnosis.

A perfectly natural explanation may be at hand for this insight. One can talk of intuition and suggest that, in the course of conversation, a score of little hints are dropped by the questing soul and subconsciously apprehended by the director, and that, as these link themselves up in the mind, the truth appears.

It may be so. The element of mystery is admittedly present, nor do we think that the more a thing is in- explicable, the more of God it contains. Whatever the explanation is, its close relationship with prayer and the fact that our insight grows as our own hunger for holiness increases, have convinced us that this is a further proof that we are working with Another. The doctors of souls, in all branches of the Church, know this gift. The Curé D'Ars is said to have had it in a conspicuous degree. Even if we allow that some exaggeration may have gathered around the many stories told of his amazing insight into the souls of men and women, we are left with incontestable proof of his astonishing ability to read hearts. A man of high social rank entered his sacristy one day but declined to kneel at the penitent stool. He protested that he had merely come to discuss things. The Curé D'Ars replied :

" Oh, my friend, you have come to the wrong place; I have no skill at discussion. But if it is con- solation that you want, kneel there and believe that

D

many another has knelt there before you and has not regretted it." [1]

So he talked with him, exposed the man's own need to him, and led him to peace, admitting afterwards that from the beginning of the conversation he had diagnosed the sheer emptiness of the inquirer's soul. His biographer says :

> " It may seem very strange that a simple parish priest should have been able so instantly and decisively to diagnose the needs of his penitents. In all this there was something more than could be explained by shrewd good sense, or by what is commonly called intuition." [2]

> " It was as though he had taken his stand in the very conscience of his penitents, with clearer vision and better memory than themselves." [3]

God does not look at a man's denominational label in presenting His gifts. Thousands praise Him for this same gift in William Fearon Halliday. He responds to consecration and fidelity in soul service, wherever He finds it. His sheep know His voice in all branches of His Church, and when He speaks to them for the understanding and help of another, they are humbled by the wonder of it but dogmatic on the fact. They listen to all the arguments calculated to prove that there is nothing in this talk about guidance, and are content to say with Le Gallienne :

> " I hear, and to myself I smile,
> For Christ talks with me all the while."

---

[1] *The Secret of the Curé D'Ars*, Henri Ghéon, p. 108. (Sheed and Ward.)

[2] *Ibid.*, pp. 98 f.   [3] *Ibid.*, p. 100.

CHAPTER XII

DOES IT FOSTER IRREVERENT
FAMILIARITY?

When I consider Thy heavens, the work of Thy fingers,
The moon and the stars, which Thou hast ordained;
What is man that Thou art mindful of him?—DAVID.

The Spirit Himself beareth witness with our spirit, that we
    are children of God:
And if children, then heirs; heirs of God, and joint heirs
    with Christ.—ST. PAUL.

THERE is a significant shade of difference in the meaning of the words "intimate" and "familiar." Both imply understanding and close fellowship, but, to this core of common meaning, there is added a flavour of something else. The word "intimate" can include a feeling of courtesy and reverence which the word "familiarity" seems not to possess. Familiarity, we are told, breeds contempt. There is a cheap ring about it. It has not protected its affection with respect nor remembered, what Mark Rutherford reminds us, that courtesy is the sheath of love.

To be intimate with God is the Christian's high privilege. Jesus taught us to call God "Father" and encouraged us to speak freely to Him about the anxious cares which filch our peace. But when that precious intimacy loses its filial awe, and men affect an irreverent familiarity with God, the feelings of all truly devout people are wounded and God hides His face.

No man can trifle with reverence and remain immune

from loss.   Most great thinkers, from Plato to Martineau,
have insisted on its nurture as a necessary part of education.   It does not degrade men, as some have suggested,
but gives a dignity to human nature and proves to be a
doorway by which one may step into a larger world.
Mr. J. Ramsay MacDonald explains the greatness of
Michael Faraday largely on the ground of Faraday's
profound reverence.

But an irreverent attitude towards God is by no means
confined to pagans.   When Mr. George Bernard Shaw
told an audience at the City Temple that he had a vague
recollection of being in the place before, but not in the
pulpit, and that he might have " stood on the communion table " on his previous visit, he was subjecting
his hearers to a kind of smart impiety that is fortunately
rare.   When he went on to say, " I like to think of
my God as a young man with his career still before him.
I hate to think of God as an old man who strikes bargains
with his creatures about the salvation of their souls
or a God who has to be bribed and begged from,"
he displayed both his ignorance of the Christian religion
and his indifference to the feelings of those who believe
it.   But this kind of irreverence is unusual in a church.
The more common irreverence comes from those who
accept the Gospel and claim a special familiarity with the
Almighty.   They speak about God and His will with
a shallow facility, and seem to claim an understanding
of the Divine mind on almost every subject under
discussion.

Not that one minds a simple and natural inclusion
of God in normal conversation.   Indeed, such simplicity
and naturalness are among the highest merits that any
word of Christian witness can have, but there is the breath
of wonder about it all the time.   God is thought of,
and referred to, as a great friend, but hardly as a particular pal.

Sometimes the most striking delinquents in these
ways are popular evangelists, whose deep sincerity

none can deny, but whose deficient sense of reverence many have had occasion to deplore. Sir Henry S. Lunn, himself a Methodist, tells in his reminiscences about a Methodist minister, with great dramatic gifts, who was much sought after in Lunn's boyhood as the special preacher at anniversary gatherings and who gave " amusing and often comic lectures in the Chapel on Old Testament characters."

" Lecturing on Jonah, he described the whale as saying, ' Come in out of the wet, Jonah, we don't often have a travelling preacher in these parts.' The proposals for Abimelech's marriage to Sarah, under the false impression that she was the sister of Abraham, gave him great scope for his peculiar gifts, as also did the long wooing of Rachel by Jacob. These jests in a place of worship contradicted all my father's early training in the Church of England, and jarred on his sense of reverence. He was particularly incensed by the fact that a very old Churchman, whom he had visited and prayed with, had come to hear this popular preacher, and after listening for a while in our pew, had walked out, muttering as he passed my father, ' They told me that a Methodist Chapel was a place to get one's soul saved. I did not expect this kind of thing.' " [1]

Such preachers were always rare and have now almost disappeared. Their irreverences were forgiven because they were full of a genuine desire to do good, but their memory serves to remind us that people are sure to lose if we rob them of a sense of awe and that the Scriptures are no fit ground on which to engineer our jests.

And all this comes back to our mind when we think of guidance, expecially when we stress the guidance which considers details. Our just insistence on God's

[1] *Chapters from My Life*, Lunn, p. 12. (Cassell & Co., Ltd.)

watchful care over the smallest things must not give us
small ideas of God. Our claim to hear the voice of
God in our soul, and often to receive His counsel on
the apparent trivialities of life, must not trick us into
irreverent familiarity and make us glib in our talk of
Divine things. God is great. Before Him the Angels
veil their faces and the seraphims cry one to another,
" Holy, Holy, Holy, is the Lord of hosts; the whole
earth is full of His glory." He is without beginning
and without end. All time is but a chapter in His
eternity. In the beginning, God. From everlasting
to everlasting, God. Heaven and earth are full of
the Majesty of His glory.

All nature speaks aloud of His might. The planets
move at His command : the clouds and the thunders,
the wind and the rain, leap from the hollow of His
hand. The birds sing at His bidding; the beasts of the
field depend on Him for their food; the returning spring
cries aloud of His constant care.

No man hath seen God at any time. A glimpse of
His glory is blinding to mortal eyes. The wisest are
ignorant before Him and the holiest are of the earth,
earthy. No wonder the saints marvel at their boldness
and ask with bated breath,

" Who can behold the blazing light ?
Who can approach consuming flame ? "

The distance that divides so great a God from so small
a creature as man seems too vast and the two aspects
of the Divine nature, the Creator and the Father, the
King and the Friend, seem to fall apart and many people
live their devotional life on one aspect alone. Either
the greatness of God fills their mind and they never
come to intimacy, or God's particular care of them is so
central in their thought that they entertain cramped
ideas of His Being and worship a magnified and beneficent
model of themselves.

Now this difficulty is as old as our religion and explains some of its variations. It is not by accident that in those forms of the faith where stress has been put on the exceeding greatness of God to the exclusion, or neglect, of His personal and paternal care, that the culture of the saints and angels has maintained itself, and still forms a not inconsiderable part of devotional life. These intermediaries become a necessity to a needy soul, which feels itself almost isolated from a God so far away. As early as the fifth century we find St. Melania saying at a shrine of the Martyrs, " O ye, who have always free speech with God that loves mankind, be my ambassadors with Him that He may receive my soul in peace." What a gulf divides such sentiments from the spirit of the New Testament! Is it only the martyrs who have free speech with God? May not every child of God approach the Father with " holy boldness " and speak from heart to heart? Paul says, " According to the eternal purpose which He purposed in Christ Jesus Our Lord, in whom we have boldness and access in confidence through our faith in Him." John says, " And this is the boldness which we have toward Him, that, if we ask anything according to His will, He heareth us." The author of the Epistle to the Hebrews says, " Let us therefore draw near with boldness unto the throne of grace, that we may receive mercy, and may find grace to help us in time of need." The witness of the New Testament is emphatic that intermediaries are obstructions : that the way is gloriously open to all believing souls : that the everlasting God, the Lord, the Creator of the ends of the earth, is a Father and takes a Father's care of His child. There is need that we guard against the old error of so shaping our thought of God on the model of a business magnate that we suppose Him to be under the iron necessity of working through subordinates and leaving the care of His ordinary children to underlings. We have not so read the Word of God. He giveth power to the faint;

and to him that hath no might He increaseth strength, and He gives it with all the immediacy and intimacy of home.

But it is the opposite error to which believers in particular guidance are most prone. The friendliness of God is real to them. They feel no gulf dividing them from the Father and no need of any further aid than that all-sufficing aid given them in Jesus. They speak to God directly and believe that they are heard and understood. But sometimes one feels that their easy access to the Father's house has dulled the sense of privilege and made them think lightly of their unspeakable gift. That is why a friendly critic of the Group Movement says :

" Ask them to think further on the greatness of God. What I mean is that their God is too exclusively friendly—prayer is just talking with a friend; public worship is just a family gathering to meet Father. That will not do. Prayer is infinitely more than talking with a friend. What of adoration and worship ? What of dim eyes seeking to bear the blaze of perfect glory ? What of the searching pains of penitence ? The more I know of the prayers of the saints, the more I am sure that friendliness is inadequate. It may be that the saints were wrong, and insufficiently Christian, but I do not think so, and somehow we must find room, not only for God's approachability, but also for the unutterable glory. Indeed, I doubt very much whether the former will long call for our adoring gratitude unless the latter is growingly real to us." [1]

That is a word which the wise will be swift to heed. Little views of God beget little souls and a narrow outlook. A great view of God means a greater possibility of spiritual growth. A sense of the Divine majesty

[1] *A Group Speaks*, p. 140.   (Epworth Press.)

need not rob us of a sense of the Divine intimacy, any
more than the revelations of the telescope deny the revelations of the microscope. Both are true unveilings of
the one great Nature and both can be real and precious
to the devout soul.

The hymn which begins,

> " With glorious clouds encompassed round,
>   Whom angels dimly see,
> Will the Unsearchable be found,
>   Or God appear to me ? "

ends with this,

> " I view the Lamb in His own light,
>   Whom Angels dimly see,
> And gaze, transported at the sight,
>   Through all eternity."

And that is the true end of man—to view the Lamb,
or so much of His blazing glory as our souls can stand.
He is great *and* approachable. He is beyond the farthest
mortal eye can scan, and yet it is our present privilege
and precious destiny to know Him in reverent intimacy.
"For it is not man's final purpose to cure pain, to
throw a cloak of decency over politics and trade, to run
churches, orphanages, schools, or reformations—but
to see God." [1]

[1] *They shall see God*, T. S. Gregory, p. 5. (Epworth Press.)

TEACH ME THY WAY, O LORD,
AND LEAD ME IN A PLAIN PATH

CHAPTER XIII

BY WAY OF WARNING

The statutes of the Lord are right, rejoicing the heart :
the commandment of the Lord is pure, enlightening the eyes :
. . . Moreover, by them is thy servant warned : and in
keeping of them there is great reward.—DAVID.

ALL good things can be
abused. The most precious gifts God ever gave His
children have been put to a poor use, and sometimes
they have been claimed with no corroborative evidence
in the life of the person who claimed them. The
more precious the gift, the more painful its prostitution
has seemed. Guidance is no exception. People have
claimed it in support of actions which are utterly in-
defensible and at plain variance with an enlightened
conscience, and it would be easy to point to many sad
events in history for which " guidance " has been the
defence. No serious student of religion will fail to look
these facts in the face, and no believer in the Directing
Hand will leave himself uninformed of the dangers his
faith involves.

All great spiritual leaders have been swift to warn their
followers of this peril. Paul, Augustine, Luther and
Wesley—the foremost figures of the evangelical suc-
cession—all have have been frank about the dangers of
such a belief. Indeed, it is not without interest to study
the counsel they gave years ago, and notice its appo-
siteness to the needs of to-day. Take Wesley, for
instance. Even his opponents admitted that he was a
man of " sound sense," the last person to be betrayed
into the follies of fanatical emotionalism, and as severe
in his reasoning as a lecturer in logic would take care to

be. He had a deep faith in God's particular guidance. When he speaks about providence, he says :

"I do not say His *general* providence ; for this I take to be a sounding word, which means just nothing. And if there be a *particular* providence, it must extend to all persons and all things. So our Lord understood it, or He could never have said, ' Even the hairs of your head are all numbered ' ; and, ' Not a sparrow falleth to the ground without the will of your Father which is in heaven.' " [1]

Wesley firmly believed that chance meetings with travellers on the road were planned by God. Yet, at the same time, in his sermon on *The Nature of Enthusiasm*, he protested vehemently against the over-use, and misuse, of the current terms employed by those who sought guidance : he urged people not to live their life " looking for any particular impressions or sudden impulses on the mind " which led to courses of action unconfirmed in principle by Scripture, and he uttered a terrible warning against the pride, stubbornness, and liability to the greatest sins, of those who cut themselves off from the help of their fellows by asserting that God dictated His will to them in all things. However improbable any of these dangers may be to a devout soul who really waits on God, it is such counsel as the humble will be willing to heed. Any person armed with a little self-knowledge, and knowing the tortuous ways of the human heart, will not resent the reminder that the path which leads to clear audition with God is beset with pitfalls. It is so perilously easy to retain the confident tone when the ground of the confidence is lacking, and to seek to avoid the inner uncertainties by a little extra vehemence in expression. It cannot fail to help if we look at Wesley's warnings with an open mind, and examine them in the light of modern experiences.

[1] *Wesley's Sermon*, XXXVII, para. 28.

Undoubtedly some people over-use the word " guid-ance." They say " I am guided," when they mean " I think " or " I have an idea." This loose use of a great term cannot be too severely condemned. It savours of cant, and cheapens the whole conception of divine guidance. One way of winning from men an admission that God does indeed guide us even (at times) in details is to be scupulously careful never to use the word except in its just meaning and, hence, to prevent it becoming a bit of jargonese.

There can be no doubt either that the term is also misused in an effort, by some people, to secure for their opinions a higher respect than reason alone would allow. It is not always simple to decide if their misuse of the word is deliberate, or if they are self-deceived. But their unwillingness to discuss the topic at all, and the odd coincidence that their " guidance " is always in the line of their established prejudices, leave one definitely uneasy about the whole matter. Nor is it unknown for people to excuse a flagrant breach of courtesy on the ground of being directed from above—an excuse which only heightens the offence because it suggests that God is guilty of things which we should condemn in a man. The wide acceptance of a practical and working faith in guidance is made the more difficult, for ordinary people, by every sad misapplication of the term in this way.

Indeed, it would probably be wise for believers in particular guidance, even when they are certain of their inner constraint, not to press the word in their dealings with those who do not believe. It has the appearance of special pleading and of seeking an advantage over an-other. The other man will either give a superstitious acquiescence to a plea which he does not understand and inwardly doubts, or else it will give him occasion to deride the whole topic. Let the guided man be content to plead guidance to those who share his faith, but let him be prepared to give plain reasons to all others, lest the idea spread that the guided thing is always irrational and is the more obviously of God the more it drifts from common sense.

Believers in particlar guidance need to remember also that God's will is not in dispute in wide areas of life. Our knowledge of God's nature is such that we simply do not need to seek His will concerning many of the temptations and problems of life. A body of basic morality we already possess. It would be perilous indeed if our faith in the inner voice were to trick us into believing that we could obtain some special dispensation for a breach of moral law. However absurd the very suggestion may seem, it is well to be humble and remember from how great a height men have slipped into gross sin, because they " rationalised " the murmurs of self-will into the voice of God, and doped their conscience until it was possible for them to believe a lie.

The relationship of guidance and routine is another side of the subject which folk find perplexing. Most people have to live their life within a framework of settled duties and they can look ahead through the weeks and the months and know, more or less, where they will be, and what they will be doing, at a certain hour and on a certain day. Such conditions appear to some people to be opposed to the possibility of particular guidance, because it would require that God respect the circumstances of our life and work within them. But is such a faith difficult ? God is not a Person of caprice. If we can venture at all on belief in His detailed guidance, we can believe also that the conditions of our life are known to Him, and that He will direct us in such circumstances as we find ourselves. Communal life would be impossible if any considerable number of people disregarded their pledged word and failed to keep their engagements, even on the plea that they were instructed to do so from above. Not the least unpleasant aspect of such a course would be the suggestion that the Holy God is erratic in His will and indifferent to our plain duties—a suggestion that needs but to be mentioned to be immediately cast aside. The man who remembers how prone our natures are to seek escape from the irksome grind of dull routine will be the more careful to examine his guidance when it leads away from the drudgery of the common round. Nothing so fosters the cynicism of the world in relation to this topic than to suspect that it always leads a person to do what they want to do—jilt a girl, cut an examination, break a promise, or neglect a difficult piece of work. While it is probable that there has been vast exaggeration, and misrepresentation, in the stories told to prove the spurious character of " guidance," it presses home the importance of great care in all claims to be directed from above, for when this great word is used to cover self-seeking it is hard to estimate the harm that is done.

Another danger that demands at least a passing reference arises from the disciple's interest in coincidences, and his just conclusion that they often provide proof that he is working with Another. We have already seen cause to look upon these convergences of unforeseen circumstances as having more than a merely odd character, and feel that they may be safely treasured up as confirmations of the appointed way. What, however, we have *not* seen cause to do, and what, indeed, we could only regard as a mistake, is to develop a state of mind which is constantly ferreting for such things and looks to little happenings, of perhaps a freakish character, as being a plainer indication of the will of God than our spiritual insight. Such an attitude to life is fraught with great peril. It manufactures a petty mind. It develops crude and false ideas of the real value of things, and will let a big decision turn, not on clear thinking and earnest prayer, but on some curious concomitance of events. The coincidences that we might justly treasure, we treasure as confirmations of a course of conduct to which thought and prayer and an inner constraint have led us, and not because of any special study of " signs."

The passion for " signs " was severely condemned by Jesus, and while the signs for which some have become eager in these latter days are not the signs the Jews demanded from Him, the parallel is sufficiently close for us to weigh His words when He says, " Except ye see signs and wonders, ye will not believe." We welcome every extra indication that we are in the line of His will, but the strained search for such coincidences we definitely set aside.

Nor can we omit a clear warning against the lurking danger of spiritual pride. The claim to hear the inner voice and have secret communications from above is so bold a claim that only those who walk humbly with their God will avoid the strident and dictatorial note. An intuition is an incommunicable thing. However positively one knows by such a means, it is impossible to pass it on. The doubts that others not unnaturally feel will provoke the unwary into vehement assertion, and in such an hour the garment of humility slips off : one strays into the company of the braggarts and we lose any likeness we may have had to our Lord.

To the sublime fact of conscious guidance we *must* witness, and witness in no uncertain way. But the mere thought that we are of those few " whom God whispers in the ear," must never nurture a sense of superiority or we shall slip into the abyss of pride. The fellowship must never become a clique of prigs. Like the windswept summit of a great mountain, this faith puts us into a position which we can only hold on our knees. It has all the wonderment and exhilaration of high places—and all the peril too.

One or two other important points follow from this. Because we receive detailed guidance on some things, we must not assume that we shall receive it on all things, and we must certainly not assert that we have it when all we possess are our settled prejudices or a couple of hazy ideas. The journey is still a journey of faith. Paul never hesitated to make a clear distinction between his own judgment and the directions he had received from the Lord. He did not allow his position as an apostle to persuade him that his opinions could be construed as guidance, and his plain dealing with his correspondents at such times is a model of Christian frankness.[1] No man loses the respect of his fellows, even if he disappoints their expectations, when he says quite openly, " I do not know God's will on that matter, though I can offer a judgment of my own."

Even those who have received most guidance are swift to admit to wide areas of their ignorance. We find ourselves on the high seas with the ocean around us and the stars above. God does not dictate every turn of the steering-wheel, though we listen eagerly to His voice when it comes. He gives us full scope for the exercise of judgment, and all our resources of mind, heart and experiences are in constant employ. Like Edward III at Crécy, He will not rob His son of the chance of achieving his full dignities by taking the responsibility out of his hands : yet He watches, and neither slumbers nor sleeps, lest His word of special counsel be necessary as we steer our course by the stars. And, after all, they are *His* stars.

Let us be willing to acknowledge the leagues we have sailed on a course that was marked out by our personal judgment, and not by some clear inner word from God. We are bold to believe it was still *His* course for us. And if some other voyager on life's ocean, admiring the directness of our route, exaggerates our knowledge and supposes that we know every rock and current in the sea, let us be swift to answer him as the wise pilot answered when he was similarly flattered : " No. I do not know every rock in the ocean, but I know where the deep water is."

It is important, too, that the believer in particular guidance be patient with people who doubt his private converse with God and reject the course of conduct that he commends. It is especially important that he does not ascribe mean motives to them, and suggest that they

[1] Cor. vii. 25, 40 (Moffat).

are wilfully disobedient to the heavenly vision. It is a plain and verifiable fact that many people who oppose a spiritual movement and seek to impede its progress with all kinds of arguments do so because their own life is deeply challenged by it. But it is not *always* the case. A man may feel serious misgivings as to the method and not be making his objections a smoke screen for his moral failures, and it would be wrong to assume that all criticism is a defence mechanism. It is not dissimilar with the fruit of guidance when it is offered to other people as a common policy. Many may object because it demands more than they are willing to give in consecrated service, but the objections of others may have at their root the honest conviction that the thing is impracticable, or inopportune, or unwise. It is an hour for patience, prayer and thought. There is no contradiction in the will of God. To preserve the fellowship and avoid all suspicion of unworthy motive in the other man is a clear duty, and a true preparation for reaching a common mind. The guided disciple will find that God asks nothing less of him than that, but in a fellowship where this is given, the Divine Father may be confidently expected, in time, to show the unity of His will.

So many are the difficulties attending the effort to live the guided life, that some will despair of overcoming them all, and decide not to go on. We cannot deeply regret the defection of any who suppose that the whole thing is easy, and that, at any moment, God will tap out His precise will like an operator taps on a tape machine. But the great prize is worth all the toil it involves, and God is infinitely patient, even with His slowest pupils. Nor should it be forgotten that the spiritual discipline, the meditation and prayer, the Bible study and fellowship, have their own rich return in addition to their power to attune us to the direct voice of God.

It is particularly important that those who have been called to leadership should recognise the problems which their faith involves, and feel the extra responsibility which rests on those who have become guides to other people.

Mr. Nixon, one-time Governor of the London Hospital, was a keen Alpine climber. It was his custom always to engage his own special guide, a man in whom he had considerable faith. One day, when they were climbing together, Mr. Nixon was horrified to see his guide disappear over a precipice. He had leaned rather carelessly on an insecure fence which skirted the abyss, and the fence collapsed beneath his weight. They found his body thousands of feet below.

A guide must not be careless. He must needs work within the limitations which hedge all human endeavours, but he, of all people, must know the perils of the way and closely follow the Great Guide with whom can be no variation, neither shadow that is cast by turning. No apology, therefore, is necessary for sounding the note of warning and of looking squarely at the dangers, because it is still imperative that he, who thinketh he standeth, should take heed lest he fall.

CHAPTER XIV

BY WAY OF ENCOURAGEMENT

But if from thence ye shall seek the Lord thy God, thou shalt find Him, *if thou search after Him with all thy heart and with all thy soul.*—MOSES.

The sons of God are those who are guided by the Spirit of God.—ST. PAUL.

LET the last word be a word of encouragement. Perplexing as many of the problems are that we have met, and partial though our explanations may have been, there is far, far more to enhearten us than to make us feel cast down. In all great effort there comes a testing time, and in so great an enterprise as the living of the guided life it comes again and again.

> " Spirit, who makest all things new,
>   Thou leadest onward; we pursue
>   The heavenly march sublime.
>   'Neath Thy renewing fire we glow,
>   And still from strength to strength we go,
>   From height to height we climb."

But we do not climb from height to height without effort, and sometimes the toilsomeness of the march tempts us to shut our eyes to the challenge of the serene peak. The discipline of daily devotion may chafe us, especially in those " dry " periods when God seems to hold no tryst with us at all, but the discipline must be endured in the sure knowledge that guidance, as a normal part of life, is only possible to those who have a rich devotional background, and in the knowledge also that it is in just such periods that God is able to do most with us. Or, perhaps, we are plagued with wandering thoughts at prayer time and despair of ever attaining to spiritual concentration, forgetful that the effort to pull our mind back, however much it wanders, and focus it again on our devotions, is a good act of prayer and exercises the muscles of our will : by such efforts do we attain the power to abstract ourselves from the tattle of a railway carriage or the bawdy talk of the smoke-room and recollect ourselves in the presence of God. But there is *discipline* in it. It is a climb and not a lift. At times the voice of God seems silent, or faint, far away and uncertain. How shall we cheer our heavy hearts in such an hour ? What strain of thought will encourage us still to persist in all that makes us sensitive to the Divine will ? By what means can our flagging desires awake with their old keenness ?

Let us think of the *wonder* of it. It is not wonderful that sometimes we grow uncertain of the pressure of His guiding hand. It is wonderful that we are ever certain of it at all. He calls a worm His friend.

> " The God that rules on high,
>   That all the earth surveys,
>   That rides upon the stormy sky
>   And calms the roaring seas—
>   This awe-ful God *is ours*. . . ."

And *ours* not only as a vassal acknowledges a king, but ours in all the dear intimacies of home, so that the first business and chief delight of daily life is

> " to attend the whispers of His grace
>   And hear Him inly speak."

The *wonder* of it ! I dared not ever *hope* for such a Guide. . . . Amazing Love ! How *can* it be ?

It is part of the fate of all things precious to grow familiar and lose their first bewildering thrill. Human love. Success. Parenthood. But surely not this? Here is something so peculiarly precious that it will only prove the rule by proving the exception and, untarnished by time or familiarity, become the glorious secret of our life and we shall move among our fellows, not proud and boastful, but quiet with a great wonder. To ourselves we shall whisper in shine and shade, in calm and storm, when the beacon light burns clearly and when it casts only a fitful gleam, "*He leadeth me.*"

Then think of the *peace* of it. The great sin of many lives is worry. The saint does not worry. At the core of his heart is trust and he reasons with himself like this, "If I trust, I do not worry; if I worry, I do not trust." He does not excuse himself by calling worry a "weakness." The absence of trust he regards as a sin. "I could no more worry," said John Wesley, "than I could curse and swear."

What is the secret of emancipation from worry? How may one shed this fretful attitude to life? Live the guided life. One need not wait till all the problems that cluster round it have been solved before one tastes its inner peace. Not to feel the whole burden of responsible decision; not to find one's mind a constant battle-ground of contending forces; not to be haunted by the fear of the consequences as one anticipates some grave mistake—that is half the journey to the land of inner peace. To find oneself sensitive to the counsel of God: to feel one's power of reason and insight clarified by the light of His presence; to reach conclusions which carry with them a sense of assurance—that is to arrive at "the Canaan of His perfect love." There is still need for toil, but it is "toil unsevered from tranquillity": it is the rest that remaineth for the people of God.

Now contrast that with the strained decisions of many people who feel no co-operative help from above: tossing on seas of uncertainty and deciding, at the last, with a most unquiet mind. Sometimes their very vacillation settles the matter. "This is the only thing

I can do *now*," they say. Indecision has become decision. They drift on with a spurious sense of relief and try to convince themselves that events had controlled it, whereas, of course, their own hesitation had finally turned the scale. It is a poor fretful life and no one is really deceived by defensive bluster about being the master of their fate and the captain of their soul. We have seen through that kind of vanity. Speaking for ourselves, we would say, " We are not our own : we were bought with a price." We bow before the " Captain of Israel's host, and Guide of all who seek the land above," and we say, " In Thy will is our peace."

Think also of the *security* of it. There are five chief tracks to the summit of Snowdon. The track that begins at Beddgelert, or South Snowdon Station, reaches the summit by the way of the narrow ridge of *Bwlch-y-Mern*.

The path is safe, but there is a steep drop on either side. When the light is good one can look ahead and walk without fear. When mists wrap the mountain round . . .

The path of life, as we conceive it, is not very different. There is a steep drop on either side. On one side there is the peril of craven fear : the crippling sense of inadequacy which numbs the higher possibilities of a man's nature and robs him of the confidence which lies at the heart of all initiative and high endeavour. He feels inferior and afraid.

On the other side is the steep descent to pride. Quite clearly, the old theologians were right when they classified pride among the deadliest sins. Mr. G. K. Chesterton has cogently argued that pride is a poison so very poisonous that it not only poisons the virtues : it even poisons the other vices.[1] Pride puts a strident note in a man's voice : it persuades him to boast and brag, to strut and shout, to assert his little self and make a gospel out of " self-realisation." And the abyss is very deep.

[1] *If I were a Preacher*, p. 14.   (Cassell & Co., Ltd.)

An old saint has said, " Ridding yourself of pride is like peeling an onion : every skin you take off there is another skin beneath." The proud man may *do* things—big things. And success will feed his pride. But he stands like a showman, in the midst of all his achievements, waving a fat palm and saying, " Alone I did it."

How are both these dangers to be avoided, the steep drop to inferiority and impuissance, and the sharp fall to pride ? How are the gains of both to be conserved ? They *have* gains. The humility of one, and the practical achievement of the other, are not to be despised. Can life be lived purposefully, and with real effectiveness, and yet without egotism ? Can a man *do* things (big things, perhaps) and not be proud ? Can he be humble and not inferior ? Yes. Both ! Both together ! He can walk along the ridge of the guided life, responding to God's constant call to service, striding out of the prison of his inferior self at the commanding voice in his soul and doing things he dared not dream to do ; and, at the same time, knowing that all his strength is drawn from a divine source, he can walk with humility and say as he goes :

> " Every virtue we possess,
>   And every victory won,
>   And every thought of holiness
>   Are His alone."

The guided life is a secure life. The possibility of error still remains, for even on a mountain a man will sometimes ignore his guide or the mists may suddenly intervene and hide him from his straining sight. But how securely the guided mountaineer can travel, despite the perils of his way, in contrast with the novice who takes a rope and an ice-axe and sets out alone ! It is not a quest *of* God : it is a quest *with* God. He climbs with zest and confidence, helping and enheartening others as he climbs. But there is no egotism because his confidence is not in himself but in his Guide.

Think finally of the *achievements* of the guided life. In some senses all Christian achievement is the fruit of guidance and we must hesitate to claim a higher merit for work done at the constraint of a voice in the soul, than for work planned in a consecrated heart without that voice; planned because it seemed the Christian thing to do and carried to a great conclusion by the help of God. Sir Wilfred Grenfell has reminded us that " the way one man gets his inspiration and his power is not any other man's business or responsibility." That is true. Guidance comes in divers manners. But if there are degrees of sensitivity to the will of God (and, quite clearly, there are) and if His guidance can come in various ways, the keen Christian will want to be open to it by every means that is possible. He will study the Bible. Reason in the light of God. Give heed to conscience. Consider the judgment of the fellowship. Listen to the divine voice in his own soul. By such listening, men and women have been led to incredible achievements, the bare recital of which makes fiction tame.

Late on the night of October 12th, 1926, three middle-aged women wandered from door to door in the neighbourhood of Victoria Station, London, seeking shelter. Undistinguished in appearance, they would have excited little comment among the passers-by, but they had just completed one of the most remarkable journeys ever accomplished by women in the history of the world. Miss Mildred Cable and the Misses Evangeline and Francesca French were home at last after a journey of more than 6,000 miles from Northern China through the Gobi Desert, Mongolia, Chinese Turkestan and Siberia. It is a wonderful story of hardship and fortitude. Through brigand-infested country, over a mountain pass which rose to nearly 9,000 feet, across the region devastated by the great earthquake of 1921 and in which 200,000 people had perished, over the dry basin of an ancient inland sea, past buried cities and through the echoing streets of deserted ones, right across the dreadful

Gobi Desert in the very footsteps of Marco Polo, right
on to London by way of Central Asia and the trade routes
that cross the Roof of the World.   Cut by terrible icy
winds at one time : scorched by the burning heat at
another : plagued by flies in one dwelling, so thick that
the walls were black with them, and by bugs in another ;
sometimes hungry, more often thirsty, weary beyond
description but starting again at four o'clock the next
morning—these astonishing women went on and won
through.   Scenes, bright in the imagination of eager
archæologists, passed before their eyes in solid fact.   The
immense caves of the Thousand Buddhas, the glorious
Lake of the Crescent Moon, " the City which holds more
gods than men," the Golden Tower of Kinta, and
mountains worn into hollows just by the force of the wind.
How did they travel ?   Sometimes swung on the backs
of mules, but riding for the most part in an old cart
made by a village carpenter for fifty shillings.   Why did
they travel ?   Because of guidance : a " secret consciousness of being in receipt of Sealed Orders.   *To
proceed to the Great North-West to a place at present unknown.*"
As they went they preached.   By word of mouth and
printed page they scattered the good seed of the Gospel.
How did they survive such dangers and hardships ?
They say, " the Hand that led protected."   Learned men
have listened with amazement to their story, but their
joy does not centre in that.   To themselves they say,
" Anybody might have found it but—His whisper came
to *me*." [1]

In July 1931, C. T. Studd died.   He had reached the
allotted span of three-score years and ten and passed over
in triumph.   One of his black boys, who was with him
at the last, said, " His only word was ' Hallelujah ! ' all
the time, until his spirit left the body."   What a great
career ended that day in the heart of Africa !   The finest
all-round cricketer in England in the early 'eighties, he

---

[1] Cf. *Through Jade Gate*, Cable and French.   (Constable.)

had put aside the hero-worship of the sporting world together with the dear delights of home and had gone out as a missionary to China. For ten years he toiled there; gave away a fortune of £30,000; married a girl who agreed with him to add another vow to the marriage service (that neither should hinder the other in any work laid upon them), and only came home when his health was breaking and he was in danger of permanent invalidism. So he was led. In 1900 God had brought him to South India, and in 1913 he began that work in the heart of Africa, in the service of which he was still wielding his bat when the Guiding Hand beckoned him home. Sickness, privation, sacrifice and toil—none could kill his zest for life, his contagious humour, or his heroic faith. " God guides," he said. " There is never any doubt in one's mind when the real word of command from God comes." It was not by guess but by God. " Hallelujah ! all the time. . . ."

Not that we must suppose that guidance comes only to the missionary overseas. The life of F. Herbert Stead is the answer to that. Like Frank Crossley, of Manchester, guidance led him to the slums. Drawn away, first from a settled pastorate, then from the claims of academic study and finally from religious journalism, he found himself in a maze of contradictory counsel from his many friends.

" Amid these conflicting claims I could only cry for clear guidance from the Directing will. One day the answer came. As I knelt and prayed, there was laid upon me the mandate that I, my wife and children, should ourselves go and reside among the London Poor to serve them in every way open to us.[1]

" . . . the mandate was not, as the subjectivist is eager to suggest, the sublimated exhalation of my own judgment and desires. I am wholly ashamed to con-

[1] *The Unseen Leadership*, F. Herbert Stead, p. 11.

fess that my submission to the mandate was attended
with little or no gladness. It came, not from me.
It came from without, from above me." [1]

And to what did the mandate lead ? It led first to the
conversion of the Browning Hall Mission, Walworth,
into the Browning Settlement, and then to the most
titanic work for Peace, Purity, Old Age Pensions, Old
Age Homes, the Unemployed, Slum Clearance and better
Housing. It is a complete answer to the charge that
those who claim Divine guidance have no tender conscience on social questions. Mr. Stead asks, " Are we
not called to recognise that Jesus Himself is the actual
Savour of the World, the actual Regenerator of human
society, the actual Redeemer and Rebuilder of humanity ? " To the realisation of Our Lord's Social Saviour-
hood, the guidance of God continually led him.

Another word remains still to be said. Let no one
feel that only the great are guided. Our habit of reaching
for a classic illustration may give that false impression.
The privilege is open to all and consciously enjoyed by
many who will never be widely distinguished. God
guides more of His servants in the paths of obscurity than
He guides in the flood-lit way. It would be a grave
error to suppose *a priori* that His word will lead to the
overseas mission field or to any prominent and specialised
service at home. To most of His children the guidance
leads to ordinary duties by ordinary paths, but it ceases to
be " just ordinary " at the thought that He desired it.
That thought makes all the difference. It keeps before
us a high view of life : lifts the roof of our poor dwelling
and takes the terror from the stars. Does He not guide
me and guide me as a Father guides a child ? Nature
cannot cower me. Will He not lead you, and lead you
as a Parent leads His bairn ? The future need not fright
you. And shall we not give the more earnest heed to

[1] *The Unseen Leadership*, F. Herbert Stead, p. 14.

all those things that make us responsive to His guidance, striving above all else for a high sensitivity to His will and so, seeking and finding, follow Him *to* the end, *in* the end and *beyond* the end where

> " The Invisible appears in sight
> And God is seen by mortal eye " ?

THE END